WHO WERE THE CELTS?

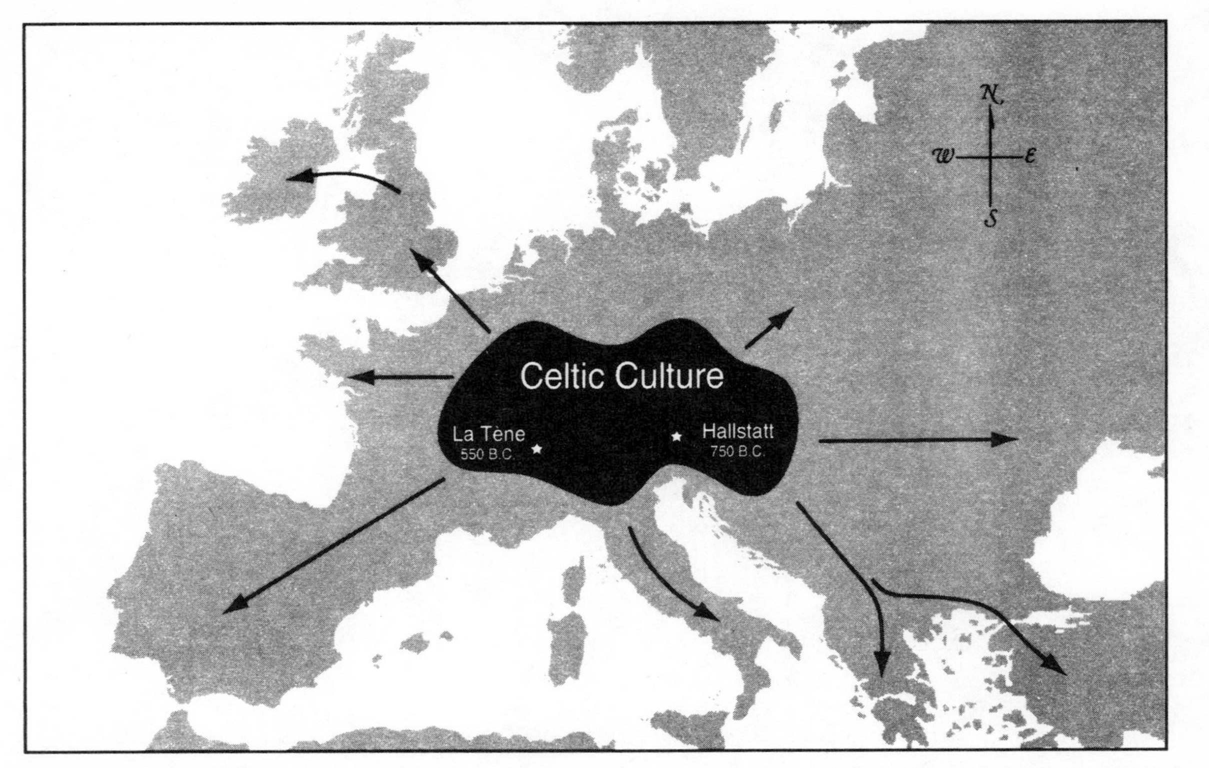

Map 1. The expansion and influence of Celtic culture across Europe. Drawn by author and compiled by Fran Stephens.

WHO WERE THE CELTS?

Everything You Ever wanted to Know About the Celts 1000 B.C. to the Present

KEVIN DUFFY

To Gerlinde,
whose contribution to this book is inestimable.

And to Alexander and Maxwell.

This edition published by Barnes & Noble, Inc.,
by arrangement with Heritage Books, Inc.

1999 Barnes & Noble Books

ISBN 0-7607-1608-0 *casebound*

Printed and bound in the United States of America

99 00 01 02 03 MC 9 8 7 6 5 4 3 2 1

RRDH

CONTENTS

LIST OF ILLUSTRATIONS

PREFACE

Events in this book span from about three thousand years ago to the present. During this time the Celts, like any other people, did not stay the same. In such territories now known as Austria, Belgium, Britain, France, Germany, Greece, Italy, Spain, and Switzerland, the Celts won and lost battles, mingled, and traded with other peoples. In 390 B.C. the Celts sacked Rome. In 279 B.C. they invaded Greece and sacked Delphi. In 43 A.D. Rome began its conquest of then Celtic Britain. Vikings later invaded and homogeneously settled among the Celts in Ireland, an island that was then additionally settled by the Normans—a century after they conquered Anglo-Saxon England in a single day in 1066 A.D.

Over the centuries the Scots, Welsh, and the Irish each evolved into unique and separate peoples. Yet it is still colloquially correct, as applied in this book, to use the adjective *Celtic* for those born or with ancestral roots in Ireland, Wales, or Scotland.

ACKNOWLEDGMENT

The author gratefully acknowledges the cooperation of Dr. Michel Egloff, and the Museum of Archaeology, Neuchâtel, Switzerland.

INTRODUCTION

There are an estimated forty million Americans of Irish descent. Countless other Americans of Celtic origin relate to Scotland and Wales. Their common ancestors, the first Celts, developed as a distinct people about 800 B.C. on mainland Europe in an area associated with the Danube basin. Archaeologists have established the location of the Celts' first known major settlement at the edge of a spectacularly beautiful alpine lake in Austria.

Most people will be surprised to discover that some of Europe's great cities, including London, Paris, Bonn, Vienna, Milan, Budapest and Belgrade, are built on Celtic foundations. At its height in 300 B.C. the Celtic realm extended all the way across Europe from today's countries of Romania and Hungary into Britain and Ireland, and from Belgium south into Portugal and Spain. Its people introduced the use of iron technology to the lands north of the Alps—the vast territories called *Celtica* by the ancient Greeks.

The Celts created the first genuine art style in Middle Europe and traded with Etruscans and Greeks centuries before there was a Roman Empire. It was an era from which the Celts would be called "the fathers of Europe." Always creative, they invented an iron ploughshare, a reaping machine, and a spoked, iron-rimmed wheel of superior Celtic design for their chariots and carts.

The ancient Celts left their mark in place names dotted all over the European map: Milan, Bologna, Rheims, Bohemia, Verdun and Dundee, to name but a few. London is made up of two Celtic words, *lug*, a god, and, *dun*, a fortress. England's Severn and Thames Rivers have Celtic names. Scotland is named after the Irish *Scotti* who settled it from Ireland. Belgium is named after the Celtic people who were called *Belgae*. Switzerland proudly takes its poetic name, *Helvetia*, from the Celtic people of that name who are ancestral to the Swiss. Paris is named after the Celtic *Parisii*. The River Seine flowing through Paris is named after the Celtic goddess *Sequanna*. Evidence indicates that the country of Germany, the German language, and the Germans themselves are named after a Celtic people named the *Germani* who once lived along the Rhine River. The name Rhine itself relates to the Celtic *renos* (raging flow), and to the Irish *rian* (sea). The River Danube (meaning swift-flowing) relates to the Irish *dana*.

The Romans introduced Latin to France's Celts, who shaped it into French. The Normans, assisted by French Celts, invaded and assumed control of Saxon England in 1066 A.D. Norman French, with its roots in a Romanized, Celtic land, enriched the English tongue and helped make it the world's major language.

Continental Europe's remaining Celts were finally assimilated by Romans from the south and by Germanic tribes from the north and east. The Celts eventually survived as a people only along the western fringe of Europe comprising Ireland, Scotland, Wales, and Brittany in France. When the collapse of the Roman Empire led into the "Dark Ages," Irish monasteries became the brightest and most active scholarly centers in Europe. Learned Irish monks in the sixth to eighth centuries A.D. left Ireland and returned to the lands of their ancestors which included Britain, France, Switzerland, Italy, Germany, and Austria. In an Irish Golden Age, they spread learning and Christianity, serving as teachers in royal courts and enriching the intellectual life of Europe. Some of the monasteries and libraries they founded in various countries survive to the present time as priceless treasures of those countries and of western civilization itself. A major Swiss city is named after the Irishman who founded it in 612 A.D. Austria has an eleventh-century Irishman as its patron saint.

During their Golden Age of Learning, the Irish developed a literature distinguished by its scholarship and original imagery. It included works written in Irish and Latin that came easily to them from centuries of learning of their scholarly bards and druids. Many priceless Irish manuscripts, more than a thousand years old, survive in the libraries of various European cities. The oldest literature in Europe after Greek and Latin, it is a part of the Celtic legacy that greatly benefited western civilization. But Ireland's monks would not be the last Celts to make history internationally.

In the year 1776 on another continent, those who signed the American Declaration of Independence included two men who were born in Scotland, two who were born in Wales, and three who were born in Ireland. Ten other signers were of direct Irish, Scottish or Welsh descent. Thomas Jefferson (of Welsh ancestry) drafted the Declaration document itself. The White House in Washington D.C. has not only been occupied by presidents descended from Celtic immigrants, but was designed and built by Irish-born architect James Hoban. Yet participation in the development of the United States of America was but a recent event in the three-thousand-year saga of the Celts....

1

The Earliest Celts

Traces of early humans in Britain go back 400,000 years. But it was not until about six thousand years ago, after the retreat of the last ice age, that permanent settlement in the islands of Ireland and Britain was commenced by anatomically modern people who would combine hunting and gathering with farming.

These early people of Ireland and Britain, possibly ancestral to the Celts, made pottery which was often decorated with elaborate abstract designs. They also built great megalithic structures, including *Stonehenge* in Britain, and five-thousand-year-old *Newgrange* in Ireland.

Among the most important of the early European megalithic structures, Ireland's Newgrange is a stupendous, hill-sized passage grave more ancient than Britain's Stonehenge. It is so designed that at midwinter sunset the entrance allows the sun to shine directly into the cross-shaped burial chamber at the end of the lengthy passage to illuminate the bones of the dead. Overhead is a corbelled stone roof. The tomb's great stones, each weighing many tons, are carved with the richest, most elaborate markings of any European megalithic structure, the meanings of which are presently unknown. Of special interest is a double-spiraled motif carved into a rock, which this writer has found to be the same design used in pieces of bronze jewelry called *fibulae* (clasps used to pin the clothes of affluent Celtic women) excavated from ancient Celtic graves in Austria and Germany. Ireland's Newgrange is located near a place called *Tara*, the seat of Ireland's Celtic high kings of centuries ago.

While it is only a theoretical possibility that the people who built Newgrange and Stonehenge were ancestral to the Celts, it is known with scientific certainty that the earliest direct ancestors of the Celts lived in an area now represented by southern Germany, Austria and Switzerland. They are called the *Urnfield* people by archaeologists because they interred the remains of their cremated dead in pottery urns before placing them in cemeteries.

From 1300 B.C. to 800 B.C. these people developed the first organized farming in northern Europe. Yet they were more than farmers. These early Celts introduced advanced techniques of bronze casting with which they manufactured such items as cast-bronze wagon wheels and finely made swords with intricately decorated handles. They used metal in making body armour and shields to complement the swords.

Efficient, creative, and hardworking, the Urnfield people formed the first affluent society in Europe north of the Alps. They lived in comfortable log cabins and boiled their meat in great metal cauldrons, washing it down with mead or home-brewed beer in bronze drinking cups. They wove bright designs into their clothing and wore metal bracelets and brooches. With their great energy, love of feasting, and their inventive skills, the Urnfielders possessed many characteristics of their Celtic descendants.

Around 800 B.C. the Celtic culture emerged among the Urnfield people. These early Celts developed as a distinct European people sharing a common material culture, language, religion, and social institutions that gave rise to the first civilization north of the Alps. In time they formed a loosely knit, Celtic-speaking, culturally homogeneous confederation of regional groups. When not at war, an activity for which they were much feared, they were prosperous farmers and cattle owners who eventually occupied much of temperate Europe, an enormous Celtic domain that would today include such places as Hungary, Germany, Switzerland, Austria, France, Belgium, Ireland and Britain.

In addition to their having inherited the renowned bronze-working knowledge of their Urnfielder ancestors, the technologically precocious Celts were highly skilled in the mining and forging of iron, a technology they introduced into central and western Europe.

With this event there evolved among the Celts a wealthy ruling class—an aristocracy—which brought a new social structure to a farming people. The development of their considerable skill in iron technology included the making of swords which were masterpieces in forging. With the establishment of these and other elements in their society around 650 B.C. the turbulent rise of the Celts commenced. It began an era in which they would dominate much of central and western Europe for centuries, an occurrence recognized in various ways by other European peoples.

The ancient Greek name for the Celts was *Keltoi*, a word adapted from what the Celts called themselves. To the Romans who came later, the Celts were known as *Galli*, a name they called the Celts of Gaul, now France. Yet Julius Caesar, who fought the Celts with his legions in Gaul, said they called themselves *Celtae*, which is basically what the Celts have called themselves for thousands of years.[1]

---

[1] Today the word *Gallic* pertains to either France or Gaul. The French, however, continue to fondly call their Celtic ancestors, *Celtes*. In Ireland, Celt is pronounced "Kelt," as in the classical Greek, *Keltoi*. But in Massachusetts they have a basketball team called the Boston Celtics, pronounced "Seltics."

First Celts In History

"We reached the deep-flowing ocean where the Cimmerians have their lands and their town. This people is hidden under clouds, in mists that the sun's rays have never pierced...."

So wrote Homer in his *Odyssey*. Some believe this is a reference to the earliest known ancestors of the Celts, the horse-riding, Indo-European language Cimmerians, a people located vaguely by the Greeks somewhere to the north of the Mediterranean.

The earliest reference to the existence of a specifically Celtic people in documented history originates from a sixth-century B.C. sea journey from the Greek colony of Massilia, today France's seaport of Marseilles on the Mediterranean coast. The account of that sea journey is now known as the *Massiliote Periplus*. The voyage took the ship through the Mediterranean's Strait of Gibraltar (then known as the "Pillars of Hercules") into the Atlantic. Greek ships must have gone that way previously, but a written account from this one specifically mentions the presence of Celts along the coasts of Spain and France. Celts in other parts of Europe must have been by then well known to the Greeks, but this is the earliest surviving historical reference to them anywhere.

In 500 B.C. Hecataeus, in describing the Greek colony of Massilia, said that it lay near the land of the Celts. He also mentioned the existence of two Celtic towns, Narbonne, now a French seaport, and Nyrax, possibly in what is now Austria, evidence that by then some Celts had developed an urban lifestyle. Such centers probably started from the grouping together of specialists in various trades and crafts in the service of local Celtic aristocrats.

In 450 B.C. the third surviving historical reference to the existence of the Celts was left to us by the Greek father of historians, Herodotus. He wrote that the Celts were living in Spain and on the Danube and that they were the most western of all European peoples, except for the Cynetes in southern Portugal. Archaeological evidence, however, shows that the Celts and Greeks had been trading goods with each other since long before the time of Herodotus.

First Historical Existence Of Ireland And Britain

The *Massiliote Periplus*, the account of the same sixth-century Greek sea voyage that is credited with recording the first historical mention of the Celts, was also the first to mention the existence of the two islands off the coast of France now known as Ireland and Britain. The account referred to them as *Ierne* and *Albion*, the earliest known names in history for Ireland and Britain. Ierne is today known as Eire (Latin *Hibernia*), and Albion survived as the Irish name for Britain for fifteen centuries. (There was also an ancient Irish people called *Erainn*). In about 450 B.C. Herodotus provided the second known historical reference to Ireland and England when he wrote of the "Tin Islands to the west of the known world from where the tin comes to us." (The tin, actually from Britain's Cornwall, was a relatively rare element essential to the making of the alloy bronze during the Bronze Age).

In about 324 B.C. (two centuries after the *Massiliote Periplus* voyage), the Greek traveller, Pytheas, referred to Ireland and Britain as the Pretanic Islands, with the Celtic inhabitants he met there being called *Pritani* or *Priteni*. A corruption of Pritania was to become the name for Britain alone. Three hundred years later, Caesar, in referring to Britain, wrote the word Pritani as Britanni or Britannia.

Although thus corrupted, the Celtic name was appropriate, for Britain, like Ireland, would continue to be a Celtic island for centuries.

Between 325-323 B.C. Pytheas personally travelled throughout much of Celtic Britain. He reported that its people were miners of tin and iron, and worked these metals as well as bronze. They were also, he said, spinners of wool, weavers of cloth and made fine pottery. He also reported that the island's Celts were pastoralists who kept large herds of cattle and sheep, and that as farmers their main crop was wheat. The climate is so wet, he said, that they must thrash their wheat indoors.

Another classical writer, Siculus, later travelled in Britain's Cornwall and apparently enjoyed a pleasant visit. He said that its Celtic inhabitants not only mined tin, some of it for export, but were civilized in their manner of life and were very fond of strangers....

To the early Romans who followed the Greeks, the misty islands of Britain and Ireland were at the edge of the known world. They believed that anybody travelling beyond Britain and Ireland—if they knew of Ireland at all—would fall off the world into a great abyss. The seafaring Celts who populated the islands apparently had no such fear. Yet there came a time when Britain and Ireland became inviting territorial targets to the Romans. No one could then have known that with a combined land mass smaller than Norway, these islands would centuries later have an effect on the world disproportionate to their size.

Appearance Of The Celts

To the people of the Mediterranean, Celtic men were remarkable for their height and muscularity, fair skin (which the Greeks praised as "milk-white"), blue eyes and blond hair—some reports mentioned red-gold hair. While not all Celts were tall, blond and blue-eyed, archaeological discoveries confirm that some were indeed of impressive stature even by today's standards. The skeleton of an ancient Celtic warrior unearthed near Milan in Italy stood six feet, five inches. A Celtic chief's skeleton found in Germany was six feet tall. In war, their stature was enhanced by their attire. First-century B.C. historian, Diodorus Siculus, wrote of the Celts that "they have bronze helmets with tall crests, which give their wearers the appearance of enormous height."

More than two thousand years ago Celtic men cultivated formidable, drooping moustaches and wore neck rings or "torcs" made of gold, silver or bronze. Consistently described as magnificent physical specimens by contemporary Roman writers, Celtic men practiced weight control, and fat warriors were fined. Pliny and others wrote of the early Celts' colorful clothing. Their cloaks could be purple, crimson, green, speckled or striped, some with ornamental fringes sewn on. The men who wore them were of haughty bearing and were said to love war and to be fearless in battle. The Greek philosopher, Aristotle, used the example of the Celts to discuss the nature of bravery. For centuries, other nations trembled at their name, yet they were known as much for their poetic ballads as for their bravery in war.

Siculus wrote that the Celtic women were not only equal to their men in stature but rivaled them in strength as well. Cartimandua, a Celtic queen in Britain, was known as a fearless leader of her people. Roman writer, Dio Cassius, recorded that Celtic Queen Boudicca "was huge of frame and terrifying of aspect...a mass of bright red hair fell to her knees." Yet while Boudicca undoubtedly made an imposing figure, it is known that classical historians were sometimes guilty of exaggeration.

Like their men, Celtic women were vain and took good care of their appearance. Using decorated bronze mirrors that were themselves works of art, they wore make-up by darkening their eyebrows with berry juice and reddening their cheeks with an herb called *ruan.* They painted their fingernails, wore finger and ankle rings, and put their hair in braids, sometimes arranged atop their heads in elaborate coiffures. They embroidered their clothing with gold or silver, and moved to the sound of tinkling necklaces and bracelets. In contemporary Rome, the poet Propertius scolded his mistress for making up like the Celts.

World's First Women With Equal Rights?

In an age when Roman wives were mere chattels to their Roman husbands (and were not allowed to own property), Celtic women were far ahead of their time in enjoying equal rights with their men. In Celtic society a woman continued to control all her personal possessions after her marriage.

Celtic women often fought alongside their men and awed the Romans with their valor and prowess in battle. Some women ruled as chiefs on their own merits (see Chapter 9). The goddess of war was but one of several important female Celtic deities.

Celts A Nation, Not A State

The ancient Celtic nation was made up of many independent chieftainships spread throughout its vast territories. Three factors distinguished its people from all others: their common language, their beliefs, and their material culture. Yet despite their oneness, the ancient Celts at no time ever constituted a single, politically unified state. This is not unusual in world history. Centuries later, when Leonardo Da Vinci was painting his masterpieces in Rome,

Italy was made up of an assortment of independent, warring states. Many of the various independent, German-speaking peoples finally came together to form a single, unified German state only at the end of the nineteenth century A.D. (to be separated and then rejoined again in the twentieth century). The ancient Celts may not have united into a single state, but this did not stop them from leaving their mark all over Europe—and even in a part of Asia.

Reaching their greatest prosperity from the fifth to the third centuries B.C., the Celts' enormous domain extended all the way from Spain to the North Sea, and from Turkey and the Russian border westwards across Europe through Britain to the windswept Atlantic coast of Ireland.

A branch of the Celts was already in Spain by the fifth century B.C. They established themselves as a ruling class over the Iberian natives on much of the peninsula. The resulting cultural blend is now referred to as "Celtiberian." They developed the two-edged sword that was adopted by the Roman legions.

The Celts Take Rome

In 390 B.C. the Celts sacked Rome, stayed seven months, and controlled it for more than forty years. A century later in 279 B.C. they invaded Greece and pillaged the sacred sanctuary of Delphi (to the ancient Greeks, "the center of the world"). The Celts never conquered all of Greece. Yet for fifty years after Delphi they held absolute control over central Europe, France, Spain and the islands now known as Ireland and Britain.

In 278 B.C. twenty thousand Celts invaded what is now Turkey in Asia Minor, settling in a region to be called Galatia, where a Celtic dialect was still being spoken five centuries later. These "Galatians" were as much Celts as were the Gauls who fought Julius Caesar in France, and the "Galicia" in Poland, and the Celts in Ireland, Britain, Scotland, Wales, Switzerland, Austria, Germany, Spain....

Like those of the Greeks and Romans, the Celtic Golden Age did not last forever. Its end in the first century B.C. came from being caught between expanding German tribes in the north and the precision Roman military machine in the south. Only in Ireland, never reached by the Roman legions, would the Celtic culture remain intact through the centuries—long after the Roman Empire had decayed and fallen to the Germans.

Golden Age Of Art

The first phase of Celtic art began from about 700 B.C. with the *Hallstatt* period dating from a place of the same name in Austria. Its finest expression dates from about 500 B.C. with the beginning of the fantastic art of the *La Tene* period, named after an archeaologically rich site discovered in Switzerland. It continued in continental Europe and in Celtic Britain, but declined with the advent of Roman conquest in the first century B.C. Today hundreds of objects in museums all over Europe attest to a brilliant and unique art that lasted for centuries, a legacy proudly shared by every country in which the ancient Celts lived.

Again only in Ireland would the centuries-old tradition of Celtic art remain intact—and survive the fall of the Roman Empire itself. Indeed the creative urge of the Celtic spirit would expand beyond the boundaries of three-dimensional art to nourish the writing of seventh- and eighth-century A.D. illuminated (elaborately decorated) manuscripts from Irish monasteries. What such Celtic scholars produced in illuminated manuscripts has never since been surpassed in world art.

Some precious and famous art objects of the ancient Irish Celts survive, such as the exquisite eighth-century Ardagh Chalice, one of the greatest pieces of metalwork of all time. Among other surviving pieces: the eighth-century Tara Brooch, the priceless, ninth-century illuminated *Book of Kells*, and the noble, tenth-century Irish high crosses sculptured in stone.

Golden Age Of Learning

During the sixth to eighth centuries, Celtic Ireland assumed an important role in the spread of Christianity and learning, sending her missionary monks and scholars to Britain, France, northern Italy, Austria, Germany and Switzerland. Today these countries still proudly possess monasteries or libraries founded by Irish scholars more than a thousand years ago. The governments of modern Switzerland and Austria are among those which include such Celtic institutions in documentary films extolling the attractions of their countries. It was a period in Celtic history that is in some ways better known and appreciated today in parts of continental Europe than in Ireland itself.

In Germany, on a bridge crossing the Main River into the university city of Würzburg, there is a statue of the Irish bishop, Saint Kilian, welcoming all those who enter. He is the patron saint not only of Würzburg, but of all Franconia. His holy day is observed every July. The Irish missionary Fridolin founded a monastery on the Rhine and is still remembered as the patron saint of Glarus, Switzerland. In 590 A.D. the Irish Saint Columbanus founded abbeys at Luxeuil and Fountaine in France. At Bobbio in northern Italy (near where Roman legions once slaughtered twenty thousand Celtic farmers and their families) he founded a monastery which is now an internationally famous center of learning. Switzerland named its eastern major city, Saint Gallen, after the seventh-century Irishman who founded it, Saint Gall. Charlemagne's court, when it was the center of Europe's greatest intellectual activity, maintained Irish scholars in residence. (see Chapter 10).

As evidence of their extraordinary vitality, the Celts left their mark in numerous place names spread throughout many countries. A branch of the Celts, the *Carnutes*, gave its name to Chartres. In England, *avon* (as in Shakespeare's birthplace, Stratford-on-Avon), is the Celtic word for river. Scotland is named after the seafaring Irish Celts called *Scotti* who permanently settled that misty, northern part of Britain. Celts settling northern Italy (two centuries before they would sack Rome) established their center at a place they called *Mediolanum* (Milan). The Celtic *Remi* gave their name to Rheims. The *Boii* gave their Celtic name to Bohemia, and invaded Italy where they also gave their name to Bologna. France's royal house of Bourbon borrowed its name from the Celtic god *Borvo*, a deity perhaps best personified by the Bourbon king, Louis XIV, who insisted on an absolute monarchy and ruled on his theory of divine right.

Industry Of The Celts

The early Celts' extraordinary energy as miners, artisans, traders, artists, sculptors and inventors contributed much to the heritage of Europe. They made roads through rugged terrain for their wagons and built ships to take them across misty seas to lands at the edge of the earth. Aerial photography clearly shows the outlines of Celtic farms in Britain dating from the Iron Age in the first century B.C. In one area in England, up to three thousand acres of fields made and cultivated by the ancient Celts have been defined. Modern Britons (as did the Romans) follow roads made by the Celts for their wagons and chariots more than two thousand years ago.

The Celts' introduction of advanced ironworking technology to northern Europe would forever shape European history. Their craft skills and technology were not surpassed anywhere until the eighteenth century A.D. In the middle of the first century B.C. these skills created an early industrial revolution that spread throughout the Celtic realm and led to extensive trade with other peoples far beyond its borders. A segment of the far-flung Celts, the *Cadurci*, operated a commercial linenworks. Two other Celtic groups, the *Gabales* and the *Ruleni*, worked silver mines. The *Sequani* Celts produced pork for export to Rome. The *Hallstatt* Celts in Austria separately mined both iron and salt and grew wealthy trading these items for wine and other goods from the Greeks and from the Etruscans of northern Italy. Gold and tin from their fellow Celts in Ireland and Britain were used by central European Celts from a vast trading network to create art and for manufacturing goods—often themselves works of art. What they did not use themselves was traded with others.

Inventions Of The Celts

In central Europe, centuries before the birth of Christ, the Celts are credited with having invented chain armour, horseshoes, the first mechanical harvester, the iron ploughshare, and the first rotary flour mill. They perfected the spoked wheel, and then invented a seamless iron rim for it so that their wagons and war chariots would ride better and further than any others. They pioneered the use of fertilizer and crop rotation and established a pattern of intensive farming that can still be traced across the countryside of Europe. Like the owners of modern hotels, the social Celts measured time by nights rather than by days—and so we still have the fortnight, a measurement of fourteen nights and days.

The Greeks credit the Celts with having invented soap. Archaeology proves that the Celts were skilled in the technology of enameling. In the fifth century B.C. they created the first genuine art style in central Europe. For a thousand years they thought of themselves as an ideal heroic society. The Celtic knight they created led to the Age of Chivalry, a social invention appropriate from a people who greatly respected their women.

The Celts and their more practical inventions led Pliny to write that their plough was greatly superior to the Roman plough of the same period. He also wrote into history that the Celts invented the mechanical harvester. He described it as a big box, the edges armed with teeth and supported by two wheels, moving through the cornfield *pushed* by an ox, the ears of corn being uprooted by the teeth and falling into the box....

It is probably no coincidence that the modern mechanical harvester was re-invented, or at least improved, by a nineteenth-century A.D. Celt, Cyrus McCormack, whose reaper made it possible for one man to do the work of ten (one of the reasons the North won the American Civil War).

The things that the Celts created were not all stylistic, utilitarian, or romantic. Two thousand years ago the most solemn of Celtic annual festivals was celebrated each year on the last night of October. Called *Samain*, it commemorated the creation of the world when chaos was transformed into order. On that night the spirits of the dead were believed to wander through the land of the living, creating a time of great danger. The Celtic-invented night of Samain and its witchery are still unknowingly celebrated two thousand years later by modern people—as Halloween. (see Chapter 4).

Origin Of "Gael" And "Gaelic"

The early Christianized Celts of Wales called their Irish neighbors across the sea by the term *Gwyddel*. The word was probably introduced to Ireland by Welsh missionaries in the fifth century when it became *Goidel*. This name eventually came to mean all the people of Ireland. From Goidel was derived the modern English *Gael*, an Irish person, and *Gaelic*, the Irish language.

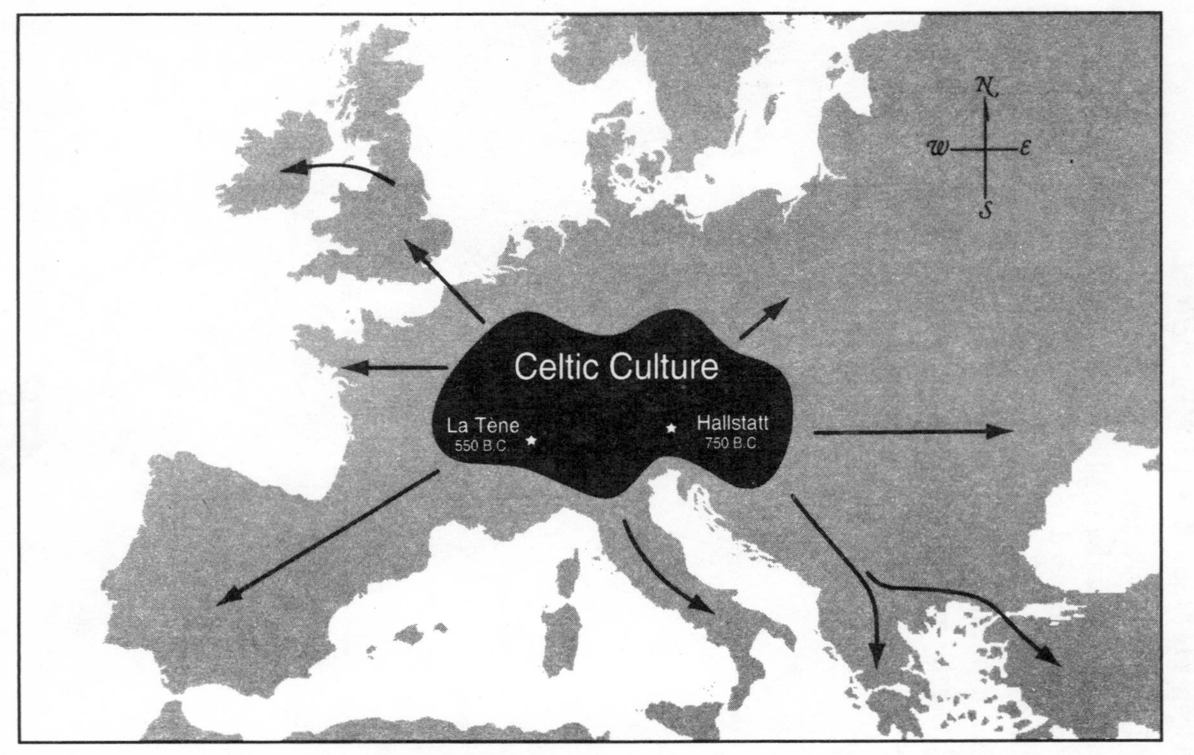

Map 1. The expansion and influence of Celtic culture across Europe. Drawn by author and compiled by Fran Stephens.

2

Ghosts from the Past

Not all discoveries from the ancient Celtic past were uncovered by archaeology. One of the most interesting events in Celtic history occurred when the body of a two-thousand-year-old Celt was found inside an Austrian alp.

The man had died violently. The place: a salt mine of prehistoric origins still being worked today beneath a mountain named Saltzberg (Salt Mountain) that towers above the picturesque, lakeside town of Hallstatt. Nearby is the town of Salzburg, itself a former Celtic settlement and the birthplace of Wolfgang Amadeus Mozart.

Found by relatively modern miners in 1734 A.D., the dead man was a Celtic miner who had been simultaneously entombed and pickled like a fish in the mine's natural salt by an avalanche about 300 B.C. If found today, the event would make world news. But in the year 1734 it remained a local affair.

The body of the well-preserved Celt was carried to Hallstatt where the superstitious villagers, judging him to be pagan and associated with the devil, denied him burial in the local churchyard. History does not record where he finally ended up. But it's doubtful if he again had a mountain for a tombstone.

It is now known that the dead man had been a member of an ancient Celtic community which in earlier centuries had occupied Hallstatt and commercially worked its salt mine since at least 700 B.C. The salt was used in local and long-distance trading with other peoples. Along with other goods,

Hallstatt, Austria. Location of the first known major settlement of the Celts. Photo by author.

A Celtic miner of about 600 B.C. with tools and backpack shown here in a museum exhibit in Hallstatt, Austria. Note the home of interlocked logs, a technique that European settlers in America would use more than two millennia later. Photo by author.

including those manufactured from their thriving iron industry, it helped to make the Celts of Hallstatt wealthy.

Now state-run, the mine, in which dramatic tours are provided for modern visitors, produces 460,000 tons of salt annually for Austria. Today the town of Hallstatt itself is a popular tourist destination. Government archaeological investigation continues in the area.

In 1846 A.D. when the "new" science of archaeology was capturing everyone's interest, the director then in charge of the Hallstatt salt mine, Georg Ramsauer, began his secondary career as a self-taught archaeologist. It all began after he made the astonishing local discovery of an extensive site containing ancient human burials. For sixteen years he excavated hundreds of graves in what was in fact a prehistoric Celtic cemetery at Hallstatt that dated from about 700-500 B.C. (The prefix "Hall" is associated with the Celtic word for salt.)

Yet Ramsauer was no ordinary grave robber. He carefully numbered and entered in a diary the details of every grave he opened. He also had an artist, Isidor Engl, meticulously draw each grave's human remains and artifacts in their exact spatial relationship as found. It was a work far ahead of its time in scientific organization. Ramsauer spent much of his own money and also somehow found the time necessary for his project despite the fact that he was father to 24 children and held his full-time job as mine manager. Ultimately, with the advent of formal archaeology, over two thousand graves of the early Celtic civilization have now been excavated in Hallstatt. This find was considered so important that the opening of one of the tombs was attended by Emperor Franz Josef.

For those who may visit Austria, Hallstatt's *Prahistorisches* (prehistoric) and *Heimat* museums have fascinating, fragile items on display, some of which have survived because of the saline conditions of the mine in which they were found. These include wooden tools, finely woven clothing, leather shoes, torches of pine to light the way, the remains of meals eaten on the job, and the framed leather sacks used to carry the rock salt for trade with other peoples. Part of a reconstructed Celtic home made of finely fitted logs is on display. Such Celtic, Iron Age dwellings were much like the log cabins that early European settlers would build in America more than two thousand years later. Proud of the Celts in their heritage, the Austrians have put on permanent display one of the best and most extensive Celtic collections of Europe in the palatial rooms of the magnificent Natural History Museum in Vienna. These artifacts of the ancient Celts were found by archaeologists in widespread locations throughout the country.

Promise Of Life After Death

From 700-500 B.C. the Celts were spread over such places as Austria, Bavaria and Bohemia. These two centuries are now collectively known to archaeology as the Hallstatt period in Celtic material culture (including Hallstatt art). Some Celtic burials during this period and up to about 400 B.C. were elaborate and even opulent, indicating the existence of a ruling hierarchy. While ordinary folk continued to be buried in simple graves with perhaps only some pottery and a sword placed beside them for use in the next world, deceased aristocrats were being buried in larger, more elaborate tombs, apparently with the concept that they could take their material possessions with them to the next life.

Such deceased members of the nobility would go on the last great adventure with more than just their sword, spears and pottery. Often placed in the tombs with them were such valuable and expensive imports as gold and amber. For their physical needs they were provided with joints of beef or pork and imported wine with which to wash them down. Future transportation needs of such very important persons were ensured by putting entire wagons and horse equipment into their tombs.

Fortunately for Celtic horses of the Hallstatt period, they were not sacrificed and sent with such equipment to the next world with their late owners. It seems that while the dead were expected to find horses where they were going, they did not count on finding the exquisitely designed metal bits and other horse paraphernalia which only the Celtic wizards of metalworking made so well.

Princess "X" Of Vix

She was only about thirty years old when she died towards the end of the sixth century B.C. in a Celtic land that is now France. Her name is lost forever. The title of "Princess" was only recently coined from the obviously affluent and regal conditions of her burial as seen by "modern" eyes 2,500 years after her death. The physical evidence clearly indicates that she was a highly regarded member of a noble and essentially wealthy Celtic family. Her large and elaborate 2,500-year-old tomb was found near the French village of Vix in 1953.

Buried wearing brooches and a large and magnificent gold diadem around her head, she had been placed on a funerary wagon in the most expensive kind of Celtic burial known. Other riches placed in her tomb included amber jewelry (imported and of high commercial value at the time), imported silver bowls, cups and an Etruscan flagon. Such exotic treasures would have represented a wondrous, royal fortune to any person of ordinary means in the princess' society.

Celtic skeleton, about 750 B.C. Austria.
Note curvilinear-designed brooch on the shoulder where it held a garment in place. Photo by author.

Curvilinear bronze brooch of a style found in Celtic graves dating to 750 B.C. in Austria. Photo by author.

Yet the Princess of Vix is immortalized in archaeology by the presence in her tomb of an object infinitely more spectacular and valuable than all of the other items combined: the largest Greek *krater* or wine storage vessel ever found. Made of bronze, with a circumference of thirteen feet, it weighs 460 pounds and is taller than the princess was herself. There is no evidence of what it was thought the princess might do with the krater on reaching the next world.

Not only the krater's size and weight was impressive. Worked into the metal are detailed images of contemporary Greek charioteers and soldiers, making it an art object of exceptional quality. Today it is thought that this enormous wine container may have been a diplomatic gift from Greek merchants to a powerful Celtic ruler to keep important trade routes open. Although finally assembled only on arrival, carrying it from Greece to the Celts in central France must have provided an epic story at the time. Once filled with wine—if it ever was—emptying it could well have provided an even more dramatic story.

The giant krater may or may not have reflected the princess' extreme fondness for wine, fatal or otherwise. After 2,500 years, no physiological evidence remains of just how she died.

Women Aristocrats In Celtic Society

Of three other extravagant burials in the Vix area, two are of women, indicating the respect with which women could be regarded in Celtic society. Also, near Hueneburg ("giant hill") in Germany—with northern France the Celtic aristocratic heartland—the same indication is given from the impressively large burial mound of *Hohmichele*. There a Celtic woman wearing the finest woven clothes, expensive glass beads and imported amber was buried on a funeral cart. That ultimate "way to go" was afforded only to the most affluent or respected in Celtic society.

Possibly a queen rather than a princess, the unnamed woman of Hohmichele may have been granted the ultimate privilege that her society could offer beyond a funereal wagon. One theory speculates that other people of lesser rank found interred in the Hohmichele mound may have been ritually slaughtered so that they could accompany their leader to the other world.

The Celtic Duke Of Hochdorf And His 2,500-Year-Old "Cadillac"

In 1977, just sixteen kilometers outside Germany's modern city of Stuttgart, a farmer from the village of Hochdorf ploughed his way into a previously undiscovered tomb of a Celtic nobleman who had died about 550 B.C. Archaeologists subsequently uncovered two underground rooms in which they found the skeleton of a powerful man about two meters or six feet tall and about forty years of age. His body had been placed on an extraordinary bronze couch or bier that was ornamented with embossed scenes of horses and dancing warriors and supported by eight female figurines, between whose feet were functional wheels or casters—as on a modern sofa. The man is today known to archaeology as "Der Keltenfürst von Hochdorf" (the Celtic Duke of Hochdorf).

His skeleton was found with a neck torc, an armband, and brooches, all made of gold. His ceremonial dagger had a gold handle, and his belt and shoes were elaborately covered with gold. The body had been clothed partly in embroidered Chinese silk, indicating previously unknown trade links. A Celtic-made, solid-gold goblet and gold-tipped drinking horns accompanied a massive, Greek-made, 400-liter or 100-gallon-capacity bronze vessel that still held the residue of the mead it had contained when placed in the tomb 2,500 years earlier.

Also found in the tomb was a fancy, Celtic-made, four-wheeled cart with multiple bronze and iron fittings that has been described as a Celtic "Cadillac." While this vehicle could hardly compare with a Celtic chariot once described by a classical writer as being made with silver rather than bronze, it was clearly intended by those closest to the Hochdorf "Duke" that he would enter the next world in the style to which he was accustomed. The priceless contents of his tomb, including the beautifully reconstructed cart and the bronze couch, are on permanent display in an impressive, air-conditioned collection of Celtic artifacts in the *Württembergisches Landesmuseum* in Stuttgart's *Altes Schloss* (Old Castle), one of that city's most central and beloved buildings.

Other Celtic collections in Germany are located in Berlin, Munich, Mainz, Regensburg, Würzburg, and Bad Königshofen.

CELTIC TREASURE TROVE

A spectacular discovery of Celtic artifacts occurred in the 1850s when the water of Switzerland's Lake Neuchâtel fell to an unusually low level. At the northern end of the lake, at a place called *La Tene*, the blackened wooden stumps of a Celtic-built bridge came into view as the water receded. The event led to the recovery of a great quantity of Celtic artifacts dating to the fifth century B.C.

Some think that flooding at this ancient lakeside settlement took its Celtic inhabitants by surprise. A more likely theory is that the objects found were votive offerings, an earlier, more religious version of the "modern" throwing of coins into fountains with accompanying wishes for essentially supernatural effects.

The water receding from the shore of Lake Neuchâtel at La Tene was like uncovering the treasures of Pompeii from beneath the volcanic ash of Vesuvius. Some artifacts lay exposed, or lay just beneath the shallow water, attracting amateur collectors. Many of the objects were collected by an antiques enthusiast named Hansli Kopp, and even more by a self-taught archaeologist of the area, Colonel Friedrich Schwab, who was probably curious about his ancestors. From 1857, Schwab spent three years dredging the site with a boat and equipment he designed for the purpose. There were coins, swords, ornamented scabbards, spears, shield bosses, sickles, knives, axes, gear for horses, pottery, and all kinds of ornaments. There would be later excavations, but the Swiss colonel was among the first.

Altogether La Tene gave up at least 2,500 weapons, utensils and other items. The discovery represented an acclaimed Celtic art form that would be produced in mainland Europe for five centuries, and in Britain and especially Ireland for a thousand years more.

*Artist's impression of the Lake Neuchâtel shore at La Tene in the nineteenth century.
Photo Du Musee Cantonal D'Archeologie Neuchâtel.*

Largest And Best Preserved Celtic Ship Ever Found

Modern divers discovered a Celtic-made, sixty-foot-long, single-masted vessel lying on the bottom of Switzerland's Lake Neuchâtel. Its builders did not merely copy a style of boat building from the Mediterranean or elsewhere. Swiss experts say that its design was spontaneously local and uniquely Celtic. Neuchâtel University and the Neuchâtel Museum of Archaeology plan to build a museum that would include in its design an underwater observation window overlooking the Celtic ship. The 2,500-year old wooden vessel would disintegrate if an attempt were made to bring it to the surface. Consequently, while it has been carefully copied, it has never been seriously disturbed.

Such a museum would be an appropriate monument to the memory of the Swiss Celts. The poetic name of this alpine country is *Helvetia,* in itself a fond recognition of the Celtic *Helvetians* who inhabited much of Switzerland in the time of Julius Caesar, and who are in part ancestral to the Swiss people.

La Tene Art

Dating from 450 B.C., the superb art found among the objects recovered from La Tene represented the beginning of Celtic art's finest expression. It was a highly original, abstract form that was not an accident in just one locality. The numerous surviving examples of this new style appear on weapons, body ornaments, horse harnesses, chariot equipment, and drinking vessels that have been excavated from sites across the entire width of Europe. Dazzling in the complexity of its design, it has been compared to modern abstract art, yet it is uniquely different, developing in a style unlike that of any other contemporary culture. Remaining unique for fifteen

1907 A.D. *excavation of* 450 B.C. *Celtic bridge* (*Pont Vouga*) *at La Tene. Photo Du Musee Cantonal D'Archeologie Neuchâtel.*

Sixty-foot Celtic boat found at La Tene. Photo Du Musee Cantonal D'Archeologie Neuchâtel.

Iron-rimmed, spoked wheel of Celtic design and manufacture. La Tene. Photo Du Musee Cantonal D'Archeologie Neuchâtel.

centuries, its integrity and continuity among the Celts in difficult times was remarkable.

Sword scabbards unearthed in Czechoslovakia, Hungary, Germany and Switzerland were engraved with the same motifs as those found in France and Britain. With impressive durability this Celtic art continued to flourish among the Celts in Ireland until the tenth century A.D. There it was used in the form of brilliantly worked metal, sculptured stone, and in illuminated monastic manuscripts.

The distinctness of the art style found at La Tene, even though it had clearly evolved from the older Hallstatt period of the Celts, demanded a new name in archaeology, and so it was to be forever called La Tene after the Swiss site where the first samples were found. A monument comprised of a giant iron Celtic sword, standing point down, its handle incorporating a human head, stands near the shore of Lake Neuchâtel at La Tene. A bronze plaque says that it marks the site that gave its name to the Iron Age civilization of the Celts. (The sword is in fact copied from one found at La Tene.)

Consequently the name La Tene represents to archaeology and the world both a period of time and its extraordinarily vigorous Celtic art style rather than just a place in Switzerland.

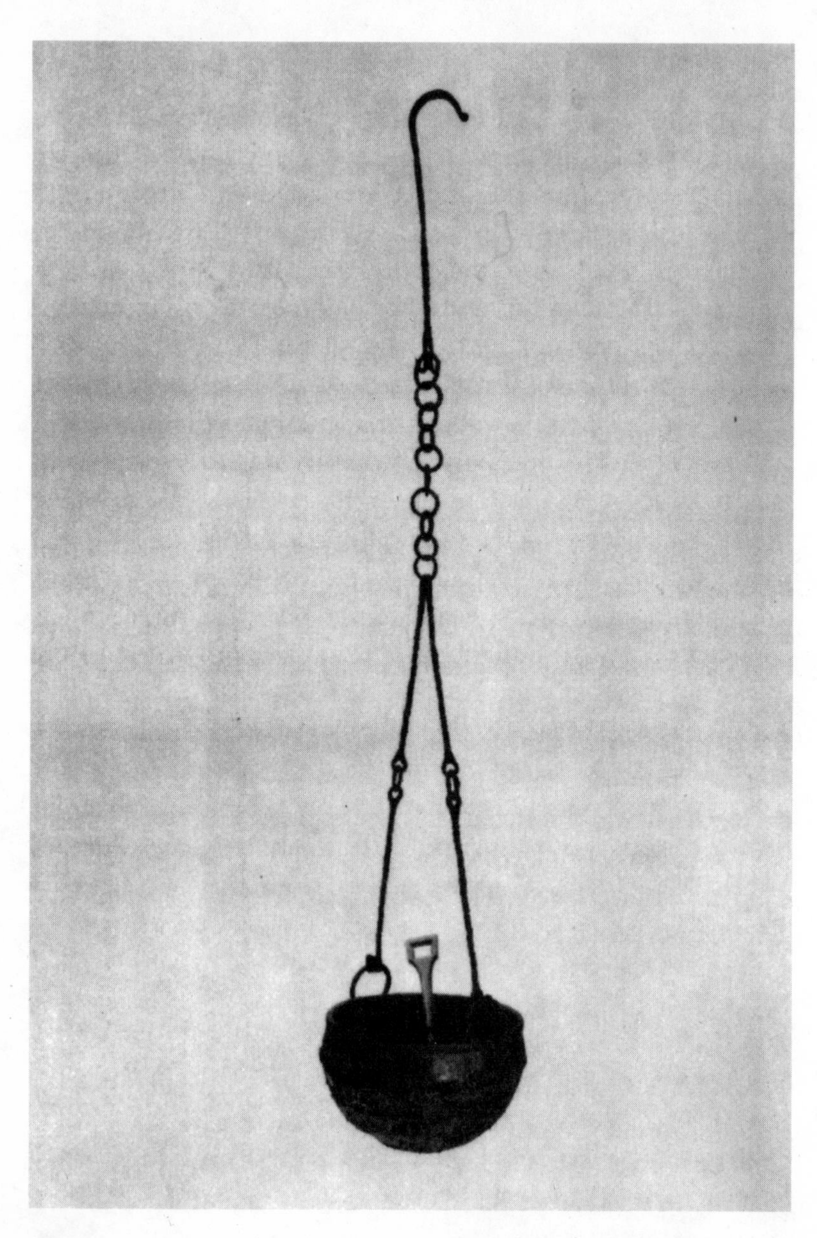

Celtic cooking pot. La Tene. Photo Du Musee Cantonal d'Archeologie Neuchâtel.

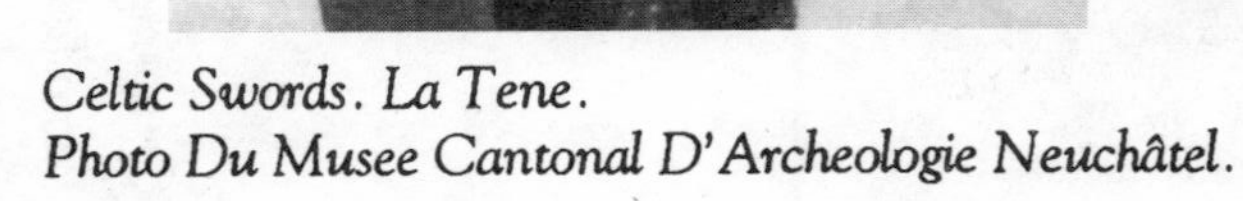

Celtic Swords. La Tene.
Photo Du Musee Cantonal D'Archeologie Neuchâtel.

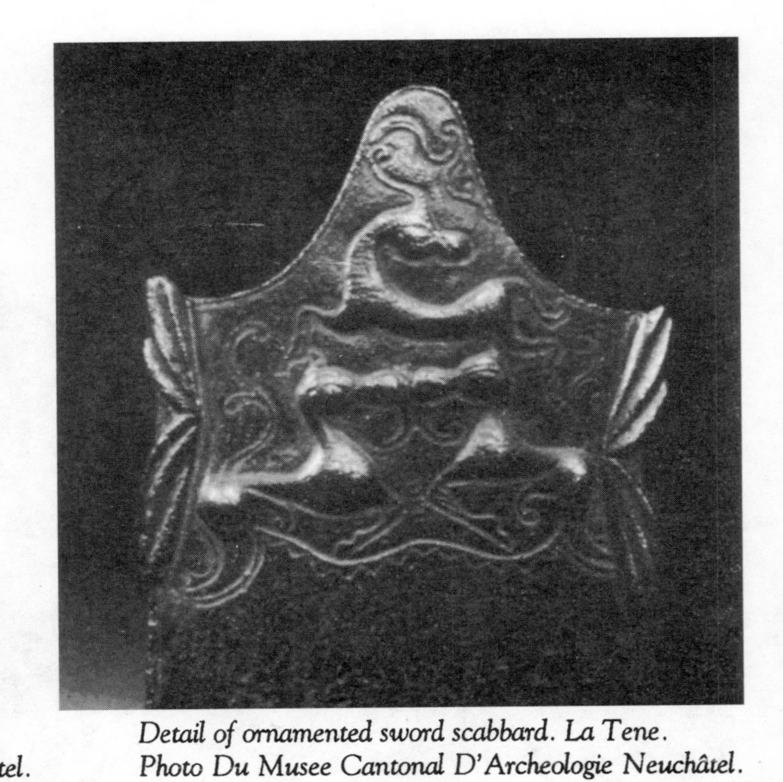

Detail of ornamented sword scabbard. La Tene.
Photo Du Musee Cantonal D'Archeologie Neuchâtel.

Celtic coin. La Tene.
Photo Du Musee Cantonal D'Archeologie Neuchâtel.

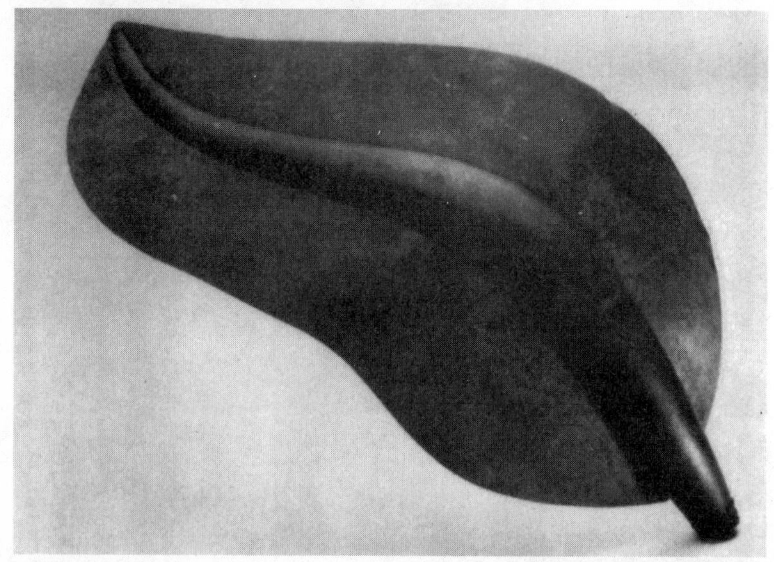

Celtic-made bronze leaf (Second-Third Century B.C.) La Tene.
Photo Du Musee Cantonal D'Archeologie Neuchâtel.

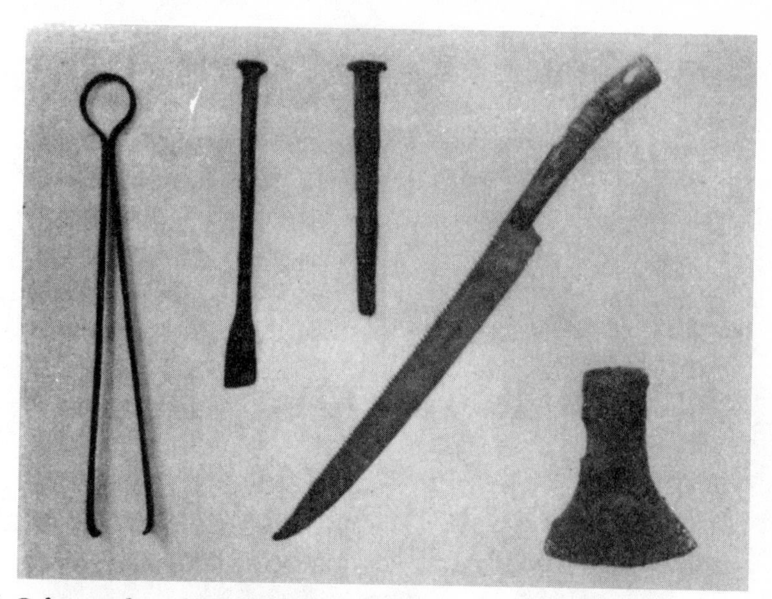

Celtic-made tools found at La Tene.
Photo Du Musee Cantonal D'Archeologie Neuchâtel.

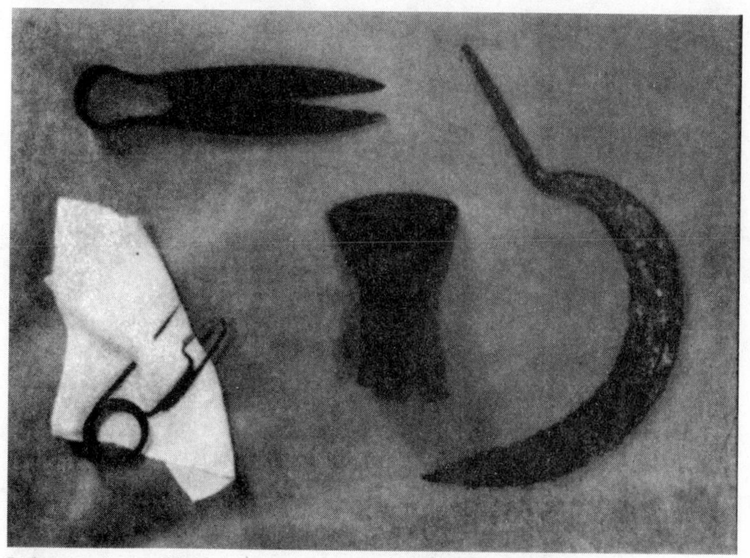

Celtic tools, including an early Celtic safety pin. La Tene.
Photo Du Musee Cantonal D'Archeologie Neuchâtel.

Bronze head of young Celt found at Prilly, Switzerland. First century A.D. Courtesy Bernisches Historisches Museum, Switzerland.

Fall Of The Aristocrats

The era of Celtic dynasties and their "princely" tombs lasted from about 650-400 B.C. It ended when Celtic society apparently rebelled against the perpetual squandering of its wealth by a privileged few—the non-working aristocracy.

A popular import of the Celts during these centuries was wine from Greece; an item much desired for Celtic banquets. Although only for the palates of the nobles, the wine was always acquired through the sweat of working Celts who must have spent an appreciable part of their lives—and their society's total energy—in maintaining its steady supply.

The burying of gold and other valuable imports in aristocrats' graves also caused a strain. The practice represented the periodic, permanent loss of a society's wealth. By being buried with the dead, such treasures could not be redistributed through the generations.

From about 400 B.C. the material goods found in Celtic burials varied little in value from grave to grave. There would still be kings and queens among the Celts for centuries to come, but the former economic gulf separating the rich from the not-so-rich had apparently narrowed to a mere gap. From then onwards, leaders were chosen by vote and not by lineage. The internationally renowned Celtic banquets, however, perhaps featuring mead more often than wine, would continue for many centuries more.

The Celtic Banquet

"Two of the things the Celts most valued," Cato the Elder wrote, were "glory and wit." And there would have been no better place to appreciate these human attributes than at a traditional Celtic banquet.

These festive occasions particularly attracted the attention of the classical "historians" who naturally tended to focus on the most sensational aspects of Celtic life, even if their information came only from the secondhand observations of others. Yet the Greek and Roman writers probably felt that they could comment with some authority on the subject since their own societies were renowned for banquets, some of which, if occurring today, might be thought of more as wild parties that sometimes became orgies.

The Celtic banquet was often a ruler's way of returning at least some of society's hard-won material wealth back to the people. At the same time it could have been a way to celebrate the presence of important visitors, or to mark a political coup, or a victory in war. Perhaps, as in modern society, any excuse was reason for a party.

Athenaeus reported approvingly that the Celts had a cleanly, if voracious, way of eating. Servants placed food on low tables, while the guests sat on cured skins or mats of woven rushes scattered on the earthen floor. A minstrel played a harp-like instrument and sang tragic songs of love and of death in battle. A professional bard entertained by singing or reciting the oral traditions of their people. When not playing the part of oral historian, the bard sang in praise of the host's bold deeds, or, for greater entertainment, instead chose to satirize the host or other noble worthy of his attention. The Celts have had a passion for poetry, song and music since the beginning of their existence. Dancing figures and a lyre have been found on seventh-century B.C. Celtic pottery from Hungary.

The banquet typically included pork or beef boiled in large bronze caldrons, accompanied by fish, bread, honey, butter and cheese, along with game such as venison and wildfowl. Wine was served to those of higher social or economic status, while the ordinary people drank beer made from wheat, passing it around in a common cup. Athenaeus also noted that each person drank only a mouthful at a time, adding, however, that they did it "rather frequently."

Diodorus Siculus reported that strangers were welcomed at Celtic banquets, and that only after eating a meal were the strangers asked who they were, and of what they stood in need. Otherwise the etiquette of precedence and hospitality was politely observed.

Nobles and others were seated according to strict protocol, their importance at the banquet measured by the distance they sat from the most illustrious guest, who would be seated next to the host. The Greek historian, Posidonius, as quoted by Athenaeus, wrote that the chief or king chose who would receive the choicest piece of meat: the boar's thigh. In the "heroic" society of the Celts this was the portion traditionally reserved for the bravest hero present.

The greatest historically recorded banquet given by the ancient Celts was provided by Louernius, a Celtic king in France. He built a one-and-a-half-square-mile enclosure in which "he filled vats with expensive liquor and prepared so great a quantity of food that for many days all who wished could enter and enjoy the feast prepared, being served without break by the attendants."

Festive banquets of affluent Celts, as recorded by Greek and Roman classical writers more than two thousand years ago, essentially required a productive and efficiently organized social and economic system. This in turn required fortified, central areas for each of the numerous groups of Celts spread throughout Europe. Two thousand years ago the Romans called the Celtic fortified centers *oppidas*. Until then probably considered impregnable, the Romans would eventually devise ways to overcome them in France and Britain. Remains of Celtic oppidas can today be seen dotted across Europe: from the once Celtic island of Britain all the way to the Black Sea at the edge of Asia.

Hadrian's Wall, the Tower of London, the Maginot Line, the Great Wall of China, the Berlin Wall...they all became just as vulnerable to change as the oppidas of the ancient Celts.

3

UNCOVERING ANCIENT CELTIC CITIES

Celtic Troys And Great Untold Stories

Homer's epic story of Troy is known today only because someone wrote it down, and because this writing happened to survive. Countless stories of gripping adventure and heroic endeavour have been lost to the world forever because the early Celts did not record their history in writing. Even when they successfully sacked Rome in 390 B.C., it was the Romans who recorded the Celtic victory for posterity. It will never be known how differently that and other stories would have been told if the Celts wrote their own history.

In 1985, Britain's BBC TV produced a fifty-minute film, "*Decoding Danebury*," which takes a look at the work of Oxford University's Professor Barry Cunliffe and his team of archaeologists who excavated and investigated the 2,500-year-old Celtic hillfort of Danebury in Hampshire, England. In a description given with the film, now distributed internationally for educational purposes, this Oxford University team found that Danebury provided "a picture of Celtic society that is every bit as rich as the cultures of ancient Egypt, Greece, and Rome."

Troy was less than five acres in extent—so small its location remained unknown for centuries. In contrast, some of the ancient Celtic communities were enormous. Britain's Maiden Castle occupied an area forty-five acres in extent, and Stanwick, Yorkshire, although not all enclosed, took up 850 acres. In France there was Bibracte near Autun with a walled area of 335 acres. The relatively tiny settlement of Troy could have been placed as a mere suburb in any of the larger Celtic centers.

One of the Celtic cities existing in 100 B.C. Germany (and destroyed about a century later) has been meticulously excavated for fourteen years by archaeologists. Strategically situated at the junction of two important trade routes in what is now Germany's Bavaria, the city of Manching was a part of the Celts' far-flung network of similar trading centers and settlements dotted all the way across eastern and western Europe. Many such centers were the beginnings of modern cities such as Budapest, Basel, Orleans, Paris and London.

Manching, however, was never rebuilt after its destruction, thus escaping the fate of later being covered over by modern cement. Today a village takes up only a small part of the land it once covered. In Manching, and Danebury, and at other such sites, archaeologists have unearthed details of an early Celtic lifestyle reflecting an even more developed and sophisticated people than indicated by some classical historians writing about people and places they had never personally seen.

Prosperous Urban Celts

In the countryside surrounding Celtic urban centers were the farms and log cabin homesteads of their Celtic owners. Inside the protective wall of Manching, the orderly streets were lined with the stone and timbered buildings of Celtic craftsmen and merchant traders. Celtic traders, if not travelling abroad themselves, sold their goods to foreign traders in exchange for coin currency. They also bartered for amber from the Baltic or for wine, coral and other exotic goods from the Mediterranean lands south of the snowy Alps.

The Celts did not trade empty-handed. Manching possessed 160 storage silos containing wheat grown by its supporting local farmers and their efficient iron ploughs. Finely made bronze, copper, iron, colored glass, painted pottery, enameled goods, bracelets and jewelry, were produced by specialist Celtic craftsmen for a local market and for export—as were smoked or salted meats, tanned hides, and furs from the European forests. Traditional Celtic medicines and herbs, used by the Celtic clergy and referred to by classical writers, were also a trade item. Slaves, kept by the Celts just as they were by classical Greeks and Romans, may also have been regularly used in trade.

Silver and gold coins were minted in Manching—and kept safely behind doors secured with Manching-made doorlocks. The first Celtic coins, however, were struck in Transylvania, Romania. (They would lead to the later minting of Celtic coins elsewhere that are now considered to be miniature works of art.)

In its time, Manching was fortified by the building of a great stone and earth rampart seven kilometers around. Three hundred tons of nails (essentially hand-made) provided by the artisans of the city's iron industry are estimated to have been used in the construction of the rampart's wooden supports.

The rampart was a defensive device commonly used throughout the Celtic domain. Julius Caesar, impressed when he encountered such structures in France, called them *murus Gallicus* (Celtic wall). Often the settlements or *oppidas* protected by such walls were built on hilltops and are today called hillforts. To the Celts they were urban settlements (surrounded by their farms) which served as centers for religion, trading, and when needed, for defense.

Celtic hillforts were once the landscape's most imposing structures across thousands of square miles of ancient Europe.

Manching in Germany was just one such Celtic walled city. Bibracte in France was a Celtic center for as many as three hundred thousand people. Its ironworkers were on the edge of the town, while jewelers and enamelers were located in houses along one of the main streets. There was a marketplace where farmers from the surrounding countryside could sell their products.

Much of the Celtic fort called *Dun Aengus* still stands dramatically on Ireland's west coast, its back guarded by a sheer cliff rising out of the stormy Atlantic.

Two-Thousand-Year-Old Arrow That Killed

Maiden Castle is the name given to the remains of a great hillfort in Dorset, England. In 300 B.C. Celts dug a moat-like trench around the site twenty feet deep and fifty feet wide. The excavated soil was hoisted to build a wall above the trench twice as tall as a man and twelve feet thick. Timber was used extensively to reinforce the wall and to build towers above the fourteen-foot-wide gates. Foundations of buildings within the wall still exist. Some areas were paved with flint cobblestones.

This fort in Dorset may have seemed invincible, but only until Roman times. The recently excavated skeleton of one of its ancient defenders now lies in the Dorset County Museum. Still lodged in one of the vertebrae is a heavy arrowhead, or bolt, which had been fired from a powerful Roman *ballista* or siege engine. This Celtic Briton was the victim of a Roman attack led by Vespasian in 42 A.D.

Prosperous Farmers

Over the centuries, the ancient Celts, while often associated with the building and use of fortified centers like Manching, continued to live as farmers.

Most practiced mixed farming, with domesticated animals—cattle, goats, sheep, and pigs—providing meat and dairy products. But cultivated crops of wheat and barley were staples. To these were added oats and rye as these species were developed, as were early forms of beans and peas. Nuts and fruits, perhaps slightly cultivated, along with honey, from both wild and domesticated bees, would be added to the menu. Honey and wheat were used in making beer or mead. Imported wine would have been available only to the most wealthy Celts.

While the Celts were among the most advanced agriculturalists of their time, they liked to regularly supplement their diet of cultivated foods with game animals and plants that grew in the wild.

Hunting, A Favorite Celtic Sport

The early Celts who lived in such places as Manching loved to hunt and fish. They lived in a Europe that had remained virtually unchanged since the last Ice Age. Waters ran sparkling and pure all the way from their loftiest mountain sources to unpolluted seas. Great forests stood where today there is none. Available to the Celtic hunter were wild cattle (the *aurochs* seen in the twenty-five-thousand-year old prehistoric cave paintings of Spain and France), three species of deer (red European, roe and fallow), boars, bears, fish and birds.

Hunting the wild boar for food was considered a sport by the Celts and is a popular theme in their mythology. Religious veneration for the boar did not inhibit the practical Celts from preferring its meat above all others for their banquets which so captivated the attention of classical writers.

If the boar was preferred by the Celts above all other wild creatures, the dog was without doubt their favorite household animal.

Celtic Dogs

The Irish wolfhound, the world's tallest dog, is of venerable ancestry and may be descended from the "swifthounds" used in war by the ancient Celts of mainland Europe, a breed known to classical Rome as *Canes celeres* or war dogs. Irish wolfhounds became known to the Romans as *Scottici canes*, or Scotti dogs, after the Celts of Ireland whom they called Scotti and who developed and bred them. The Roman consul Quintus Aurelius Symmachus received a gift of seven Irish wolfhounds. They ended up on display at the Circus in Rome where the crowds were as fascinated with them as they would have been with any exotic animal. Dogs were used by the Celts when they invaded Greece in the third century B.C., their success in part attributed to using dogs as a kind of shock troops against the Greeks. Some Celts at that time trained their dogs to proceed in advance of their infantry and hurl themselves on the enemy who would use up their spears on them and become demoralized.

In the fifth century A.D. Saint Patrick wrote of obtaining a three-day passage on a ship sailing from Ireland to Gaul (France) which was carrying a cargo of hunting dogs. Such dogs were especially popular in the hunting of the wild boar. The breeding of hunting dogs in Celtic Britain and Ireland was considered an art. The breed now called the English bulldog was found by Caesar in the distinctly Celtic Britain of 54 B.C., centuries before the first Englishman existed. Ironically, this dog would become the symbol of English grit and, draped by cartoonists in a Union Jack, of the British Empire itself. Until 1835 bulldogs were used by the English in the "sport" of bullbaiting, an amusement involving the setting of dogs on bulls tethered in an arena.

Besides the aristocratic Irish wolfhound, selective breeding has since produced various species of "Irish" dogs—including Irish setters, terriers, and water spaniels. The Irish wolfhound is at its best in a rural setting. Despite its great size, however, it is known to make a surprisingly adaptable house pet, being gentle, affectionate, and good with children.

The Celts have long been associated with the domesticated dog. Their sculptures, more than two thousand years old, show that the Celtic goddess of the forest was always accompanied by her hunting dogs. While the dog was indeed popular with the ancient Celts, it was, however, the horse with which they can be said to have had a centuries-long love affair. They even had a goddess of horses.

THE CELTS AND THE HORSE

Probable Origins

It is possible that the steppes of Russia and eastern Europe represent the most distant, traceable place of origin for the people who evolved into the Celts. Like the horse-riding Cimmerian and Scythian people associated with that region, the ancient Celts spoke an Indo-European language, and from the beginning were renowned for their skill as horsemen.

The goddess of horses, *Epona*, was an important deity to the Gallic Celts of France. Sculptures of the period show her decorously riding a horse side-saddle, sometimes accompanied by a foal or a bird or a dog. Celtic reverence for the horse extended to Britain where the horse goddess was called *Riannon*, and to Ireland where she was known as *Macha*.

The famous Celtic, second-century B.C. *Gundestrup Cauldron* (found buried in Denmark) shows central European

Celtic soldiers in battle blowing long trumpets, the ends of which are shaped like the heads of horses (some say boars).

World's Biggest Horse

Probably the most extraordinary representation of a horse anywhere survives intact at the site of a first-century B.C. Celtic fort at Uffington, England. Three hundred fifty feet or 110 meters long, it was carved into a chalk hillside, and can still be clearly seen from twenty miles away. Its Celtic artists may have regarded it as the symbol of a horse goddess.

In contrast, the smallest horse representations are those found pulling chariots on Celtic gold coins. One such coin, from first-century B.C. France, is now in the possession of the British Museum, London.

A panel of the Gundestrup Caldron, made by Celtic craftsmen in silver more than two thousand years ago and found in Denmark, portrays a goddess and her attendants.
Photo by James P. Blair, © 1977 National Geographic Society.

Another panel of the Gundestrup Caldron features the Celtic horned god Cernunnos in his world of animals.
Photo by James P. Blair, © 1977 National Geographic Society.

A third panel of the Gundestrup Caldron shows Celtic horsemen wearing crested helmets, warriors with shields, and others blowing animal-headed war trumpets. Speculation of the meaning of the two figures on the left include the scenario of a slain warrior being revived by submersion in the sacred cauldron of the god Dagda.
Photo by James P. Blair, © 1977 National Geographic Society.

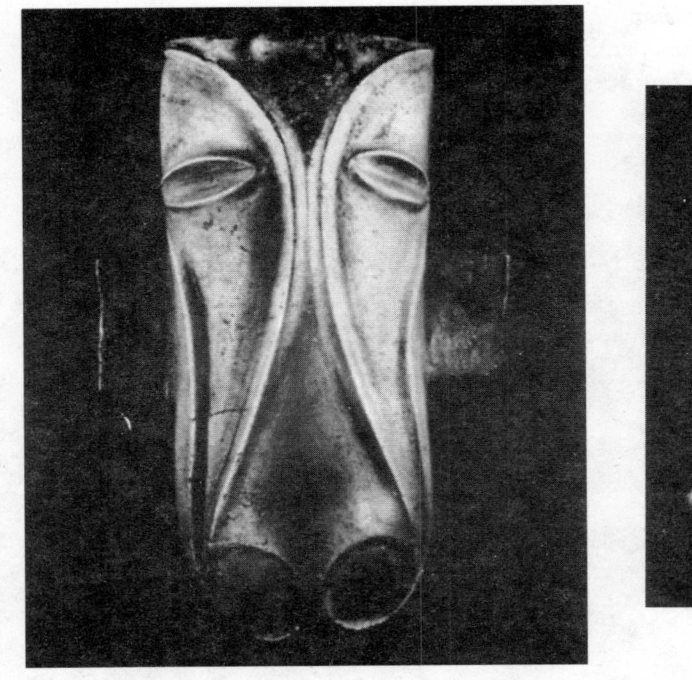

Bronze horse head ornament. From Celtic Britain.
Photo by James P. Blair,
©1977 National Geographic Society.

The Celtic iron and bronze Amfreville helmet.
Recovered from the River Seine, France.
Photo by James P. Blair, ©1977 National Geographic Society.

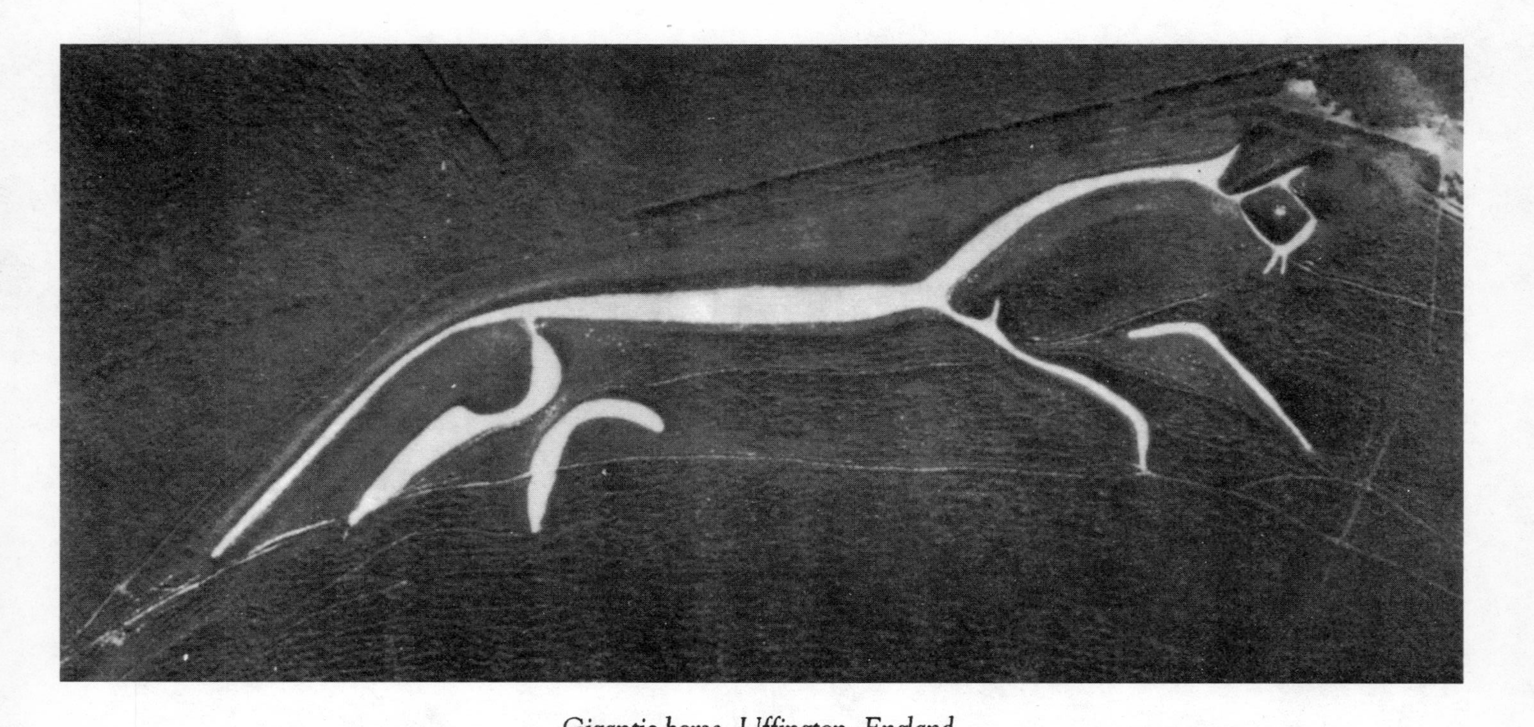

Gigantic horse, Uffington, England.
Three hundred fifty feet, or one hundred ten meters long, and visible for twenty miles.
First century B.C. Celtic Britain. *Photo by James P. Blair,* ©1977 *National Geographic Society.*

The Horse In Art And Competition

Numerous archaeological finds from across Europe testify to the dedication with which Celtic artists produced art in fine metalwork for the aggrandizement of the Celtic nobleman, his horse and for his chariot. It is improbable that the fine art found in horse-related equipment was created just to impress the enemy in battle. There was ever a rivalry between clans and local chieftains to surpass the others' high standards of craftsmanship. Annual parades and chariot races, along with other competitions and festive occasions, provided the opportunity to proudly display the valuable skills of the artist. Celtic warriors from mainland Europe in about 400 B.C. brought with them to Ireland the sport of chariot racing. The aspirations of those times are reflected today at the annual, international *Dublin Horse Show*, Ireland, where traditions in the pursuit of excellence in horsemanship continue.

Because it made more dramatic copy, classical writers tended to dwell on the military aspects of the Celts and their horses. Yet horses were used for many things in Celtic life—farming, weddings, funerals, annual pageants and international trading. In time of peace the Celts were a nation of horsemen. Only in time of war did they become a nation of cavalrymen who terrified the infantry of the Greeks and Romans.

Four horsemen inscribed on a sword scabbard from the Hallstatt period indicate that, by the end of the seventh century B.C., fighting from horseback was already known to the Celts. Thus a tradition began that would endure until the sixteenth century A.D. in Ireland; a continuum of well over two thousand years—an existence longer than Christianity itself. It's little wonder that horses are in the Celts' blood.

The archaeological evidence also shows that by the end of the seventh century B.C. the lance was already a favored weapon of the noble Celtic horseman (just as it would be centuries later for his legendary descendants, the Arthurian, Celtic knights in their defense of Britain against the "barbarian" Anglo-Saxon tribes after the departure of the Romans).

Earliest Account Of Celtic Cavalry In Action

A rare fourth-century B.C. description of Celtic cavalry in action was written by a contemporary Greek named Xenophon who was himself a cavalry officer. He recorded that Celtic mercenary troops were sent from Syracuse to help the Spartans in the war between Sparta and Thebes. "Although they were few," he wrote admiringly, "the speeding Celts on their horses manipulated the entire Theban foot army, compelling it to advance or fall back at their will."

Some Celts hired themselves out as mercenaries to foreign powers such as the Romans, the Greeks, and the Egyptians; including the pharaoh Ptolemy II Philadelphios who ruled Egypt from 283-246 B.C.

4

Who Were Those Druids?

No pre-Christian system of religious belief seems more mysterious to modern people than that of the ancient Celts and their *druids*. As priests of the Celtic religion, the druids had many duties related to annual festivals surrounding the agricultural cycle. Four of the most important celebrations included:

Imbolc, the feast of renewal and purification celebrated on February 1 and dedicated to the pagan goddess *Brigit* (who, with the advent of Christianity, became known as Saint Brigit);

Beltaine, celebrated on May 1 with prayers for bountiful crops in the face of unpredictable northern weather;

Lugnasad—festival of fertility or first fruits (later called *Lammas*), celebrated August 1.

As for the fourth festival, not many know that the celebration of *Halloween* on October 31 is a perpetuation of a two-thousand-year-old annual religious festival of the Celts called *Samain*. Dedicated to *all* the gods and denizens of the Celtic *otherworld*, it commemorated the creation of the world when chaos was transformed into order.

On that night various supernatural entities, including the spirits of the ancestral dead, were believed to wander among the living, creating great danger. It was customary to put food outside dwellings to appease related but not necessarily friendly spirits who were thought to have the desire to sit once again at the family hearth with their living descendants. This important occasion, dedicated to all the Celtic gods and ancestral spirits, was eventually renamed "All Saints' Day" and "All Hallows' Eve" in adjusting to early Christian beliefs. Today millions of children innocently roam their neighborhoods in the darkness of Halloween night wearing scary masks with the expectation of being given things good to eat. They are unknowingly representing the spirits of the dead, playfully threatening homeowners with dire consequences if they are not given a treat on demand.

Although the druids were mentioned by Aristotle in the fourth century B.C., their existence was first historically recorded in some detail only at the beginning of the second century B.C. among the Celts of Gaul (France). About 150 years later Julius Caesar, after years of war, finally succeeded in destroying the culture (and "druidic" religion) of the continental Celts. By about the end of the fourth century A.D. the Celts remaining in Britain and Ireland had become Christianized.

All the druids on earth had thus ceased to exist more than one thousand years before Columbus "discovered" America. Yet today millions of people on various continents are immediately familiar with the name druid—and what they think it means.

Just What Was A Druid?

Druids were the learned priests of the ancient Celts. Julius Caesar wrote that they "officiate at the worship of the gods, regulate public and private sacrifices, and give rulings on all religious questions. Large numbers of young men flock to them for instruction, and they are held in great honor by the people. They act as judges in practically all disputes whether between tribes or between individuals."

Druids were also considered to be natural scientists. Cicero credited them with having a great knowledge of physics and astronomy (which they used in making complex five-year

Celtic calendars). From Pliny we know that the druids were responsible for preserving the medical knowledge of their people. They were thus teachers, healers, judges, poets, priests and—reportedly from studying suitable omens during sacrifices—augurers or foretellers of the future.

Like modern clergy, druids were exempt from paying taxes and from military service. The remarkably well-preserved body of a two-thousand-year-old Celt, known to archaeology as *Lindow Man*, was recently found in a peat bog near Manchester, England. It is thought to be the remains of a druid, in part because of the body's well-manicured, unblemished hands. Even socially important, non-laboring Celtic bards would show calluses from years of playing musical instruments, and the hands of Celtic aristocrats would show the effects of riding chariots, fighting, and hunting. The druids were known to work only with their minds.

Origin Of The Word "Druid"

To the ancient Celts the oak tree had mystical, sacred properties, and Pliny has suggested that druids were named after it. The Sanskrit word for oak is *druh* (the Celts spoke an Indo-European language). The Greek word for an oak tree is *drus*.

It is also possible that the word "druid" was derived from parts of two words. The first syllable, *dru*, still emphasizes the importance of the oak tree. The second syllable could have been derived from the Indo-European root *wid*, "to know." The meaning of the combined words could be interpreted as "knowledge of the oak."

"Trees of knowledge" and "trees of life" are symbolic of religious spirituality in many cultures. One of the first was the date palm, sacred to Osiris six thousand years ago. The Indian tree, Asvattha (*Ficus religiosa*), sheltered Gautama Buddha as he sat beneath it while reaching what Buddhists think is the perfect state of the human mind.

Romans And Celts: Traditional Enemies For Centuries

For hundreds of years Rome was a nation at war with the Celts, a people whom the Romans could never forgive nor forget for sacking their city in 390 B.C. Only after losing against the Celts for generations did the Romans finally develop their legions of professional career soldiers to conquer the unprofessional farmer volunteers of the Celts. The Romans eventually subjugated the Celtic peoples in such territories as those now called Italy, Switzerland, France, and Britain.

History is written by the winners, and consequently much of the material written by the Romans on the Celts was naturally biased and sometimes fabricated. Romans writing on the druids in particular did so without ever meeting or even seeing one. They depended for much of their information on a Greek writer, Posidonius, who visited what was apparently Gaul in the second century B.C. and who produced uncorroborated material on what may have been drudic activity there.

Thus it was from Posidonius' writings (long since mysteriously lost and existing now only in the form of fragmented interpretations by others) that some Roman writers derived their total knowledge of the Celtic druids. Their secondhand "reports" (written years and even centuries after the events) were often luridly sensational and presented in much the same style as the material presented in certain modern tabloids about aliens from outer space or re-appearing Atlanteans. Roman "historians" using Posidonius as a source for their writing on the Celts (and/or their druids) are said to be of the "Posidonian tradition."

Only Those With Good Memories Need Apply

Although some druids could read and write Latin and Greek, it was traditional that each one should commit to memory not only the entire religious teachings of their people, but their laws, history, and folklore as well. Caesar wrote in the first century B.C. that "their religion forbids them to commit their teachings to writing...although they use the Greek alphabet in nearly everything else, in their private and public accounts."

The druids did not form a closed or hereditary caste. Initiates were accepted from the community at large provided they could survive the strenuous training required—Caesar said it took twenty years. Only young men of good intelligence were accepted. Often they were of the Celtic nobility.

The vast body of knowledge that the druids had to learn was put in verse for easier memorizing and for passing on from generation to generation as an oral tradition. It would not be until the fifth and sixth centuries A.D. that some of this unique knowledge would be transcribed and permanently preserved in writing by Irish monks.

Like millions of people today, the ancient Celts were confident of the soul's immortality, and Caesar was one of these who wrote that the Celtic religion incorporated such a doctrine. Pomponius Mela remarked that such was the Celtic belief in life after death that "some even used to defer paying debts until their arrival in the next world."

Immortality may have been a subject of special interest to Julius Caesar, since he claimed descent from the goddess Venus.

Power Of The Druids

According to Caesar, decisions or judgments by the druids were absolute and final. "Any private person or any tribe refusing to abide by their decision is excluded from the sacrifice. This is the heaviest punishment that can be inflicted; for those so excluded are considered to belong to the godless and wicked."

The power of the Celtic druids extended far beyond their own community. As a pan-Celtic institution they could arbitrate disputes between chieftains or kings. Siculus (who called the druids "song-loving poets") said that they were even known to walk between opposing armies and stop a battle before it started.

Each year representatives of the order of druids from all across Gaul met in assembly with their archdruid leader at Chartres, named after a branch of the Celts and now the site of a world-famous cathedral. There, among other business, they arbitrated both private and intergroup disputes. The archdruid was chosen on merit and appointed by vote of his fellows.

More than two thousand years before the invention of mail or telephone services, druids were in contact with each other all across the vast Celtic territories. Caesar said that the druids of Gaul communicated with the druids in Britain—from where he thought druidism originated. It has since been suggested that the druidic religion originated in Ireland, a place that came to be known to classical writers as *insula sacra*—the sacred island. Whatever its origin, druidism was a considerable intellectual force which helped to bond the Celtic people into a whole. At the height of Celtic influence a druid could travel all the way from Asia across Europe to Ireland without stepping off Celtic territory.

Three centuries later, Caesar's future in Rome depended on his defeating the Celts in France, by then the Celts' last stronghold on mainland Europe. Aware that the druids were at the core of rebellion against his legions, he determined to eliminate any members of their order he might find. These learned priests had the potential ability to organize the Celtic nation into a single coordinated force—a force he knew could be invincible. Like other Romans after him, he felt that to defeat the Celts he must destroy their druids.

Yet the future dictator of Rome did not really have to worry on this account. Although the druids were national and even international in concept and power, they would never achieve their full political potential because theirs was a cultural rather than a nationalistic force. In resisting Caesar, these non-combatant scholars were merely attempting to protect their culture and people from his deadly legions.

The Druids In Classical Retrospect

Not everything the early historians and writers said about the druids was unkind. Diodorus described them as "philosophers and theologians." Strabo gave them credit for their "knowledge of moral philosophy and natural science." Hippolytus credited them with a knowledge of Pythagorean calculations. Julius Caesar attributed to their learned priests "much knowledge of the stars and their motion, of the size of the world and of the earth...."

By the time Caesar had been dead for three hundred years, Greek scholars in Alexandria had decided that the druids had actually been great "moral philosophers." By then the druid priesthood of the Celts had been described as many things, from most bloodthirsty to most wise.

The Calendar Of Coligny

In 1897 A.D., near the French town of Coligny, archaeologists found the broken remains of a Celtic calendar. Made in the form of a bronze plaque, it measures about five feet by three and one-half feet. Dating to the first century B.C., it is the oldest surviving document in the Celtic language and is now in the possession of the Musee de la Civilization Gallo-Romaine, Lyon, France.

Although using Roman lettering and numerals, it is written in Gaulish (the Gallic or Celtic language of ancient France) and is purely Celtic in nature. It contains appropriate Celtic festivals and auspicious and inauspicious dates suitable for various events such as planting, harvesting, bringing in the herds, etc. Using a system clearly predating the Roman occupation of Gaul, it owes nothing to the Julian calendar of Rome.

A masterpiece of calendrical calculation, this invention of the Celtic druids covered a five-year cycle, with an indication that parts of it may have involved a nineteen-year cycle. The Celts estimated time by nights, not days, and nineteen solar years are almost exactly 235 lunar months. Cicero, a renowned Roman scholar who was born 106 B.C., wrote that the druids were great natural scientists who had a knowledge of physics and astronomy applied in the construction of calendars.

Human Sacrifice

Probably the worst thing the Romans felt they could claim about the druids was that they practiced human sacrifice—even if much of what they thought they knew about the everyday life of the Celts was based on frequently second-hand, biased, and unconfirmed reports. The occurrence of human sacrifice, however, would not have been too surprising in the world of two thousand years ago. For centuries, Rome itself was no stranger to human sacrifice. Although finally abolished by senate decree of 97 B.C., each year countless numbers of people continued to be cruelly killed in Rome for the entertainment of spectators. Men and women (including a known Celtic man and woman) were ritually buried alive in the Forum Boarium. This unpleasant practice continued into the first century A.D.—a century after Caesar had destroyed much of the Celtic culture (and its druids) in Gaul.

Rare Eyewitness Account Of A Druid Ceremony

To the Celts, mistletoe was a popular healing plant that could be found growing parasitically on the bark of oak, hawthorn, lime and apple trees. It was considered to be at its most potent, however, when found growing on an oak tree. With its highly sacred character, mistletoe was especially associated with the druid priests.

Pliny the Elder (23-79 A.D.), one-time Roman procurator in Gallic France, claimed to have witnessed the harvesting of such a plant. What he wrote, however brief, may be the nearest thing that the world will ever have to an original, firsthand account of an actual druidic ceremony. It occurred in about 50 A.D. among what was left of the druidic order in France after Caesar's eight years of war with the Gallic Celts a century earlier. The ideal location would have been beneath an oak tree in a grove of sacred oak trees.

It was appropriate, Pliny indicated, for the mistletoe to be harvested on the sixth day of the waxing moon. On the appointed day a pair of white bulls was brought to the site. A druid in a white robe then climbed the tree and cut through the stem of the mistletoe with a gold knife. Others below caught the valuable plant on a white cloth. The two white bulls were then sacrificed as a propitiatory gesture to a god (who was thought of as an unseen observer but who was not identified by Pliny). Prayers were offered to the god to make the mistletoe strongly effective as a medicine.

Pliny would later write that he thought mistletoe was an effective cure for sterility (whether for his own or for that of others will never be known).

Mistletoe

People paid the druids for pieces of the plant, believing that it kept witches away. Centuries later in eighteenth-century Ireland, Christian priests forbade the mistletoe to enter their churches; yet it not only got in, but found a place over the altars where it was held to betoken good will to all mankind. The *Country Magazine* for 1792 included the useful information that "a custom of kissing the women under the mistletoe-bush still prevails in many places, and without doubt is the surest way to prove prolific."

The practice of kissing under mistletoe is said to have originated with the Celts. Along with Pliny's suggestion that mistletoe was good for sterility, it seems that the plant has always incorporated the qualities of a mystical aphrodisiac. Even today it is known in Gaelic as "all-heal."

The ancient Celts and their descendants had good reason for their belief in the healing powers of mistletoe. Recently, Swiss, German, and American researchers found tumor inhibition in excess of fifty per cent, in mice that were treated with juice expressed from this plant.

The mistletoe widely sold in America is *Phoradendron flavescens*. In Europe the "true" mistletoe, *Viscum album*, is most popular. The mistletoe species, *Phoradendron serotinum*, is the state flower of Oklahoma. Using modified roots, the parasitic mistletoe plant with its waxy white berries and evergreen leathery leaves grows on the bark of various host trees. Christian monks believed that it was the plant that originally formed the wood for the cross of Jesus and could never again touch the ground; hence its need to root only on the bark of host trees.

Druids And Witchcraft In Britain

Owen Glendwr, a Celt of Wales, was said to have used magic in fighting for Welsh independence against the English. Born in 1349 A.D., he was educated in London where he was called to the English Bar. Colorful and exceptionally intelligent, he came to the notice of the king, became part of the royal court, and was knighted at age 38. He later fought the English for Celtic independence in Wales, where the English claimed they were repeatedly thwarted in battle by his magic (which was thought to be derived from druidic knowledge).

Glendwr is uniquely looked upon as spiritual ancestor by some of the witchcraft cults practicing in modern Britain. Belief in the existence of witches, who can be male or female, is common throughout the world. It is known that Solomon had recourse to one. In England, the last court trial for practicing witchcraft occurred in 1937. In 1989 the American state of Rhode Island officially granted tax-free status to a coven of witches as an authentic religious organization.

The "Romantic" Druids

Archaeological findings and the Romantic movement spurred a rediscovery and interest in the Celts from the seventeenth to the nineteenth centuries. Numerous countries, all the way across Europe from Hungary to Germany, Switzerland, France, Britain, and Ireland, could legitimately claim the ancient continental Celts as ancestors.

Subsequently a folklore developed around the Celtic druids that imagined their roles in Celtic society as ranging from fierce anti-Roman champions of liberty to repositories of mysterious wisdom; to worshiping in stone circles (especially Stonehenge) surrounded by oak trees and mistletoe, to being early patriarchal Christians and prophets. The nineteenth-century Russian theosophist, Helena Blavatsky, who believed in reincarnation, even claimed that the druids were "the descendants of the last Atlanteans." Belini wrote the internationally renowned opera, *Norma*, with the main characters as druids (Norma's father being the archdruid). It has been performed at La Scala since 1831, in recent times with an impressive "megalithic" stage setting. Featuring the priests of the ancient Celts in high opera was just one sign that druids were becoming acceptable and even fashionable after centuries of obscurity.

The words druidess and druidism were invented only in the eighteenth century A.D. There is now even a word for the study of druids—druidology. From the 1700's druidic societies were set up in London and elsewhere. As a young man Winston Churchill joined the *Ancient Order Of Druids* in 1908.

National Heroes

National pride in a Celtic heritage does not always acknowledge the druids directly. The modern Belgians (whose country is named after the Celtic *Belgae*) have erected an imposing statue of the Celtic chief, *Ambiorix*, at Tongres. While presumably Ambiorix had druids at his court, they are not included in this recognition. But others have been more thoughtful.

The English accept the Celtic King Arthur as a larger-than-life, legendary Briton who fought valiantly against the

Saxon invaders of Britain (even though the Saxons in part became the English themselves). Merlin, the king's magician, seer and teacher in the legend, was clearly a druid by any other name.

In France there is a "Wine of the Druids" bottled by a vineyard called "Chateau of the Oak." Also in France, in recognition of his country's fascination for their Celtic ancestors, the famous nineteenth-century forger, Vrain Lucas, fabricated several "Celtic" letters. Lucas not only forged letters from Celtic chiefs, but he created one that was supposed to be from Lazarus to Saint Peter which included a discussion of druids.

All this leads nicely to "Asterix," the French slapstick comedy that is one of the most popular cartoon strips in the world, being published in twenty languages. Set in Gaul (France) in 50 B.C., its characters include the physically diminutive Celtic hero, Asterix, and the druid, Getafix. With other ancient Celts they are in a constant (and usually victorious) feud with an imperious Caesar and his legions.

Stonehenge And The Druids

Popular present-day belief holds that the Celtic druids built the great structure of Stonehenge in Britain. Archaeological evidence indicates, however, that it was built by an earlier people than the Celts and their priestly druids. Yet the belief persists.

When one of Stonehenge's giant upright stones fell in 1900 A.D., the monument's modern owner at that time, Sir Edward Antrobus, decided to restrict entry to this megalithic wonder. He built a fence around it and began to charge for admission. All went well at Stonehenge until the next solstice when a modern, self-proclaimed "chief druid" had to be removed by the police. The ejected "druid" later publicly and ritually cursed Sir Edward.

Sir Edward quickly sold Stonehenge for 6,600 English pounds to a Mr. Cecil Chubb, who then promptly got it off his hands by presenting it to the state in a ceremony attended by "druids." Since then, official records show that numerous British groups, thinking of themselves as "druids," have applied for permission to perform their rituals and ceremonies at Stonehenge. Others attempt to temporarily occupy the prehistoric megalithic wonder without permission and are arrested.

Organized, generally peaceful, modern "druids" gather annually in a mystical dawn ritual among the giant stones of Stonehenge to celebrate the summer solstice. A Mr. George Reid (who incidentally stood—unsuccessfully—for both the U.S. Senate and Britain's House of Commons), was Chief Druid from 1906 to 1946.

Modern would-be druids will be pleased to know that since the ancient astronomical computer that is Stonehenge employed a base of nineteen years to bring solar and lunar years into synchronization, there could indeed be a link between this megalithic wonder and the Celtic druids, since the two-thousand-year-old, Celtic-made Calendar of Coligny uses the same nineteen-year base.

Celtic built or not, it is possible that Stonehenge knew the presence of real druids and their rituals two thousand years ago in a Britain that was then Celtic. Within its great stones, druids might even have celebrated *Samain*, the festival that would become Halloween. It will never be known how the druids in Britain may have dressed while performing their rituals. Modern would-be druids at Stonehenge perform in ghostly white robes as described in *haute couture* detail by Pliny the Elder in his eye-witness account of a druid ceremony two thousand years earlier.

Modern children wear their own scary costumes on Halloween, unaware of the original Samain festival and its association with the spirits of the dead. The ancient Celts and their priestly druids would be flattered to know that something they started more than two thousand years ago is being perpetuated by millions of people all over the world—even if these same millions don't quite know just what is being celebrated.

ROME AND THE SUPERNATURAL

Rome's High Gods

If the little that the Romans knew about Celtic religion seemed strange to them, it was hardly less bewildering than the religious beliefs of the Romans themselves. To the Romans, there were two triads of "high" gods, the first being composed of *Jupiter*, *Mars*, and *Quirinus*. The second triad, the main focus of Roman veneration, has Jupiter enthroned as the central figure with the goddesses *Juno* and *Minerva* flanking him on either side. The month of March is named after *Mars*, the Roman god of war.

Rome's Lesser Gods

The Romans had gods for almost everything. These were not only amazing for their number, but also for their variety. *Janus*, after whom the month of January was named, was the god of gates and doors. Incredibly, an old gate in the Forum was considered to be Janus himself—probably the first and last gate to be a god in the history of the world.

Terminus was the god of boundaries, to whom the blood of countless animal sacrifices was offered annually by farmers and others in the hope of keeping harmony between neighbors.

Cloacina reigned as the goddess of sewers, especially of Rome's largest, the *Cloaca Maxima*, which drained the Forum into the river Tiber. It is not known if the river god, *Tiber*, objected to Cloacina's pollution of his domain.

Romans believed in these and many other gods for centuries—right up to the beginning of Christianity—long after Rome had vanquished the last independent Celts and their druid priests in continental Europe.

5

Who Were Those Romans?

The history of the early Celts was dramatically linked with the Romans for centuries. The first notable event between these two peoples was nothing less than the sacking of Rome by the Celts in 390 B.C. Thus began a relationship that would endure until the fall of the Roman Empire, eight hundred years later.

Legendary Beginning Of Rome

In Roman legend, twin brothers *Romulus* and *Remus*, sons of the god Mars and a mortal princess named *Rhea Silvia*, were abandoned as infants by being set adrift in a basket on the River Tiber. Floating safely to the bank, they were suckled and cared for by a she-wolf. Eventually they were found and raised by a shepherd and his wife.

Romulus was chosen by omen over his brother to be the one who actually founded Rome in 753 B.C. He also became its first king. The site chosen for Rome was at the place where the brothers as babies had been rescued on the bank of the river. Remus became an enemy of his brother and was killed for mocking the city's fortifications. "So perish whoever else shall leap over my walls!" Romulus boasted.

The distinguished Roman historian, Livy (59 B.C.-17 A.D.), wrote that Romulus bolstered the meager population of Rome by making it a sanctuary for fugitives from the surrounding countryside; according to Livy "a miscellaneous rabble...eager for new conditions." He obtained wives for them by leading "the rape of the Sabine women;" the Sabines being a neighboring people whose women the Romans ravished. After a long reign Romulus disappeared forever in a thunderstorm and was subsequently worshiped by Romans as the god Quirinus.

Until the advent of Christianity centuries later, all Romans believed that Rome's founders, Romulus and Remus, were descended from a celestial father, "none other than Mars." Under future kings this early Roman monarchy extended its territory in all directions by means of constant warfare—until its rule was taken over by its northern neighbors, the Etruscans (see below).

Real Beginning Of Rome

The foundations of Roman culture were established long before the building of Rome itself. From the eighth century B.C. numerous Greek colonies were established throughout Italy and Sicily, some not far from where Rome would one day stand. Some continued to exist in Italy after Rome was established. The region of Italy and Sicily was then called *Magna Graecia*, "Great Greece," and to this day it contains the remains of more Doric temples than there are in Greece itself.

There can be little doubt that the Greek presence had an effect on the developing culture of the *Latins* living then on the south side of the River Tiber in an area called *Latium*. Yet these pastoral folk, who would one day build Rome, were probably already speaking an early form of Latin and not Greek. It was their then more powerful neighbors to the north, the Etruscans, who were the most important outside influence involved in the spectacular rise of the Latin farmers to be the world's greatest power.

The Mysterious Etruscans

It is not known where the Etruscans came from before founding a civilization in what is now Italy. Just north of where Rome would one day be built, the Latins would come to know the region as *Etruria* (now Tuscany and Umbria).

The Etruscans' civilization began in the eighth century B.C. when Rome would have been a simple village if it existed at all. It reached its political peak in the sixth century when it became a great sea power and established colonies as far away as Spain. It declined in wealth and power in the fifth and fourth centuries B.C. (With their culture decaying, and further weakened by their own civil war, the Etruscans would eventually cease to be a political entity by 88 B.C.) These people remain a mystery because their origin has never been established, and because scholars have been unable to relate Etruscan to any other language known on earth. Their precise relationship to the Celts and other people will probably never be known. Their superb art, however, offers no mystery and is considered comparable to the best of classical Greece.

Until about 500 B.C. the Etruscans occupied much of Latium and ruled Rome itself. At that time the Latins, now called Romans, overthrew their Etruscan overlords to subsequently establish the Roman Republic in 509 B.C. with Rome as its center. This is generally considered to have been the date of the real founding of Rome, the city built on seven hills.

The founding of Rome thus took place *after* the development of the Celtic culture, or about 250 years after the establishment of the Celtic mining and trading center at Hallstatt. Then, as now, that former Celtic settlement, in what is now known as Austria, lies separated by the Alps from the Mediterranean peoples.

Celts In Italy

During the fifth century B.C. a wave of Celtic expansion from beyond the Alps brought a branch of the Celts to settle in northern Italy. This was a relatively peaceful migration resulting from a natural population increase. In Italy they not only continued their existence as efficient and prosperous farmers, but founded the city of *Mediolanum* (later Milan). Polybius wrote of the Celts in Italy's Po Valley, describing their homesteads and neat fertile fields of wheat, barley, millet, vines, and figs.

After 400 B.C. the Celts had so prospered and grown in number that some of them began to migrate further south into Italy in search of new land. With their fearsome long swords they overcame Etruscan armies and overran Etruria as they moved southward. Ahead was the Etruscan city of Clusium, and beyond that was the city of Rome. Livy wrote that to the people of Clusium it was a "terrible situation" as they received reports that Etruscan armies had been scattered. In desperation the Etruscans sent for help from their enemy, Rome.

Fatal Step Of The Roman Envoys

An uneasy Rome sent envoys to the Celts to negotiate peace. The Celts met them and demanded land on which to settle. What happened then is best described by Livy. "When the three envoys asked by what sort of justice they demanded land from its rightful owners, and what business Celts had to be in Etruria, they received the haughty reply that all things belonged to the brave who carried justice on the point of their swords. Passions were aroused and a fight began. It was then," Livy added, "that the envoys took their fatal step."

"The fatal step" of the envoys was not only in ignoring an international convention that prohibited them from participating in a fight, but one of them took advantage of his group's diplomatic status to actually kill a Celtic chief. Livy gives this as the reason for the Celts deciding to march on his beloved Rome in the year 390 B.C.

The Celts Sack Rome

The Celts travelled eighty miles in four days to reach Rome after the killing of their chief. Livy describes the scene as they marched purposefully southward across the land. Terrified townships rushed to arms as the avengers went roaring by; men fled from the field for their lives; and from all the immense host, covering miles of ground with its straggling masses of horse and foot, the cry went up "To Rome!"

Rome was not undefended. Its army met the advancing Celts near the city, but was quickly defeated. Livy says that the Roman officers and men alike fled at the first sound of the Celtic war cry. The Celts swept through Rome plundering and destroying as they went. They were the first outsiders to control the city on the Tiber since the Tarquin (Etruscan) rulers overthrown by the Romans more than a hundred years earlier.

According to legend the chief of the Celts exclaimed "woe to the conquered" as he added his heavy iron sword to the weights on the scales used to measure the gold tribute given by the Romans to their conquerors. It was a remark "intolerable to Roman ears," Livy would later write.

Intolerable or not, the Celts stayed in Rome for seven months, until dysentery and lack of food drove them out of the ravaged city. They returned to their stronghold in northern Italy with all the Roman booty they could carry. Polybius wrote that the Romans remained under Celtic domination for more than forty years.

Neither Romans nor Celts had any idea then that four hundred years later Rome would dominate almost the entire known world, controlling Egypt, Syria-Palestine, Greece, and all the way across a giant swath of Europe into Britain. It would not be until the fifth century A.D.—about eight centuries later—that Rome would again be overrun by invaders. In 476 A.D. the West Roman Empire would finally fall to the German Goths.

Centuries later the Goths would become better known for the use of their name in a grand architectural style, as seen in many European cathedrals, than for having deposed the last Roman emperor. Ironically, that emperor, Romulus Augustulus, was named after Rome's first ruler, Romulus.

6

Historic Encounters 335-225 B.C.

Alexander The Great And The Celts

In 335 B.C. Alexander the Great was campaigning in the area that would be known as Bulgaria. As one of history's greatest generals, he had just defeated the *Getae* and burned their capital when he received an envoy of Celtic warriors. The Greek historian, Arrian, wrote that these Celts, for whom Alexander gave a feast, were "a people of great stature and haughty disposition."

Knowing of their valor, Alexander asked the Celts what they feared most, expecting to hear that it was himself. To his chagrin they instead answered, "We fear only that the sky fall and crush us, or the earth open and swallow us, or the sea rise and overwhelm us." Since these things were unlikely to happen, it seems that the warriors were saying that they feared nothing.

Alexander and the Celts exchanged diplomatic gifts, and peace was made. But a half-century later, armies of a Celtic migration from the area of the River Danube devastated Alexander's homeland of Macedonia, killing its king and heir to the glory of Alexander. From Macedonia the Celts would divide and proceed to invade Greece along two different paths.[1]

---

[1] The Greek historian, Polybius, wrote of the relentless force of the Celts in the third century B.C., who were then a people so influential that, at the time of their invasions of Greece and Rome, separate parts of their nation were the dominant power in many other parts of Europe.

Delphi Sacked

In the mid-winter of 279 B.C. the Celtic migration under the leadership of Brennus was moving southwards through Greece looking for new land. An additional attraction lay ahead in the treasures known to be deposited in the Greek sanctuaries, among them Delphi, the most famous. Yet this was essentially a migration rather than a raiding foray, since the Celtic fighting men were accompanied by families and wagons and had no plan to return to their point of departure. Although attacked frequently by the Greeks, these Celts were well protected by Brennus and his warriors who in the manner of advancing armies were living off the land.

It was Pompeius who wrote of Brennus—after this Celtic leader had taken part with other Celtic groups in the conquering of Macedonia and was marching through Greece towards Delphi: "Then, as if the spoils of men have no further attractions for him, he turns his eyes to the temples of the immortal gods, joking that they who are rich, must make presents to men. So he marches on Delphi...."

The most sacred of all Hellenic sites, Delphi contained the shrine of Apollo and the temple of the oracle, Pythia (python), an old woman consulted by emperors, kings, and unknown numbers of lesser citizens. The Celts sacked the temple, slew the Pythia, and carried off treasures which had accumulated at the site for generations. Strabo confirms that the Celts took with them a huge quantity of spoils, and that treasure later found in the sacred Celtic lake at Toulouse came from Delphi. Scenes of the Celts sacking Delphi were later carved on the doors of Rome's temple of the Palatine.

Apollo's Revenge?

Livy also wrote about the Celtic sacking of Delphi. But it was the Greek historian, Pausanias, who left a fantastic account of the incident, saying that during Brennus' advance on Delphi an earthquake opened up bottomless chasms in the earth and, accompanied by lightning bolts, the ghosts of past Greek heroes arose. (There is historic evidence that there was a severe if not freakish earthquake accompanied by landslides and unusually harsh weather, including a snowstorm, during the Celts' advance toward Delphi through rugged mountain passes).

The gods of the Greeks were not their gods, and Brennus with his warriors were apparently undeterred in achieving their goal. Yet Brennus himself had apparently been wounded in battle and would pay the ultimate price. After leaving Delphi with his army, he heroically took his own life to avoid a lingering death from his wound that would have hindered and therefore endangered his people on the march.

Realizing that they could not hold off a combined Greek force, this particular branch of the Celts moved back north to Thrace which they held as a Celtic kingdom for 86 years. (Thrace still exists in name, but is now divided between modern Greece and Turkey).

Celts In Asia Form An Early Democracy

After the sacking of Delphi, a part of Brennus' people, joined again with two other Celtic groups who had parted from them in Macedonia, and crossed the Dardanelles into Asia Minor. About twenty thousand of these established a state in Turkey called Galatia. For more than a hundred years they wielded considerable power, receiving tributes from neighboring rulers as far away as Syria.

Volso, a Roman consul visiting the Asian Celts, wrote of the Galatians (as quoted by Livy), "They sing as they advance into battle...clashing their weapons against their shields...the Greeks and the Phrygians are scared by this display..."

However they fought in war, the Galatia Celts established a very early form of democracy. Classical historians wrote of "the commonwealth of the Galatians," describing a political system involving an assembly of three hundred elected representatives. The Celtic language was spoken in Galatia for about seven hundred years—until the fifth century A.D.

Celts In Egypt

Various pharaohs of ancient Egypt employed thousands of Celts as professional soldiers in their armies, going back at least to the four thousand Celts who served the pharaoh Ptolemy II, ruler of Egypt from 283 to 246 B.C. According to Pausanius and Callimachus, Celts even attempted, unsuccessfully, to overthrow Ptolemy II and take over his Egyptian kingdom. But Celtic soldiers were internationally held in very high regard, and a couple of Egyptian reigns later, ten thousand Celts from Thrace were employed by the pharaoh Ptolemy IV, who gratefully used them to rout the twenty-thousand-man army of his enemy, Antiochus of Syria.

Peter Ellis describes four contemporary Celtic soldiers in Egypt who provided their own unique footnote to history. In about 186 B.C. while in the service of the pharaoh Ptolemy V, these adventurous Celts, so very far from home, took time off from their army duties to inscribe their names in the chapel of Horus at the Great Temple of Karnak. In fluent Greek, they identified themselves as "Galatians," giving the Greek form of their Celtic names, Thoas, Callistratos, Acannon and Apollonios, and wrote that they had just caught a jackal (which they mistook for a European fox). Like the pharaohs, these Celtic soldiers may not have achieved immortality, but their literary effort in a fleeting moment of time will allow their names to be known forever. Ellis says that bands of

Celts with their wives and children settled in Egypt. Some of their graves have been found at Hadra near Alexandria.

North African Berbers Descended From Celts?

A theory holds that the sometimes blue-eyed and blond, non-Arab Berbers of North Africa may be the descendants of Celts, thus explaining the mystery of their origin. Like Celts of classical times, the northern Berbers are an agricultural people with a political democracy who have local industries of iron and other metals, pottery and weaving. Some Berbers formed North African states such as Mauretania and Numidia. Renowned, like the Celts, for their prowess in battle, the Berbers are said to have formed the backbone of the "Arab" armies that conquered Spain. The Berbers known as the *Tuareg* are a people among whom descent and inheritance are through the female line, and, as among the classical Celts, whose women enjoy respect and freedom. With a remarkable similarity to the Celts and their bards, some Tuareg are renowned for their sharp wit and a custom of composing songs of ridicule.

Ancient rock paintings found in the Tassili n'Ajjer mountain range nine hundred miles southwest of Algiers include some which may possibly relate to Celts who came to Africa in the time of the Egyptian pharaohs and stayed on. While people in the paintings are typically represented as dark-skinned, one ancient painting is completely different in style and content and includes four light-skinned women, one of them blond. Wearing Celtic-style capes and modern-looking hairstyles, these women are presented with dignity, indicating the regard in which they were held. It is tempting to speculate that they were of Celtic origin.

Famous Sculptures Of Celts In War

In 230 B.C. King Attalus I of Pergamum (a Greek city in Turkey) fought and defeated a group of Galatians. It was not an important battle, for the Celtic Galatians continued as a potent independent state into the next century. The event, however, has a special place in history because of a series of sculptures King Attalus had made so that his victory would not be forgotten. It was a plan that worked better than he may have originally conceived.

The most famous of these sculptures, *The Dying Gaul*, is of a wounded and naked Celtic warrior sitting on his shield awaiting the end. Another sculpture of the series shows a naked Celtic warrior thrusting a sword into his own chest rather than surrender. Genital naturalism was clearly preferred over the artifice of a fig leaf. The subjects are presented as a handsome, heroic people, but the sculptures clearly symbolize what Attalus intended, his victory over the Galatians.

Copies of the "Pergamum" sculptures were made and distributed widely among the Romans and Greeks before the originals were lost. Today, copies of both sculptures mentioned here can be seen in Rome, a marble representation of *The Dying Gaul* being on display in the Museo Capitolino, Rome. In the third century B.C. the notoriously well-dressed Celts sometimes employed bands of *gaesatae* or spearmen who were known to fight naked for religious reasons. Relatively few in number, they were professional soldiers who fought for whatever ruler wished to retain their services. The sculptures made by the Greeks of Pergamum reflect this practice, the extent of which was exaggerated by the reproduction and distribution of the sculptures, and by both classical and more modern writers. As Professor Powell (see Bibliography) reminds us, however, the custom of fighting unclothed had been widespread by other peoples in Greece and Italy.

Romans And Nudity

The Romans were apparently broadminded about nudity. Many of their male and female gods were represented by nude statues including Mars, the god of war. Being naked and well formed, he is shown as having much in common with the Greek sculptures of the Celtic gaesatae.

As indicated by painted pottery and other art forms, Bacchus, god of wine, not only went naked in public, but encouraged his mortal followers to do the same during their bacchanalian, orgiastic festivities. The god of fertility, Priapus, was perceived as having huge genitals. He is portrayed in art with an erect penis of heroic proportions supporting a considerable quantity of fruit balanced on top of it. A surviving Priapus-related representation shows a naked Roman (mortal) farmer contentedly among his cattle in the field. Nearby is a little altar aflame in honour of Priapus whose fertilizing abilities include things grown on the land.

One public ritual involving nudity, the *Lupercalia,* is famous for having been incorporated by Shakespeare in his play, *Julius Caesar.* In it naked young men in Rome run around flicking with whips any women they see. It was believed that "the barren, touched in this holy chase, shake off their sterile curse."

Skirts And Trousers

If the extraordinary gaesatae of their time sometimes fought naked, ordinary Celtic warriors dressed for battle. While the Romans wore the skirt-like toga, the Celtic cavalry and infantry wore trousers, colorful cloaks, and tunics with gold or silver-plated belts around their waists. Because of their peoples' skills in various crafts, the Celts could be found elaborately adorned not only with fine and even fancy clothing, but also various kinds of body armour. The oldest complete specimen of chain mail ever found was excavated from a third-century Celtic grave in Romania. Fragments of garments with protective rings of metal threaded into them have been found in an even earlier, eighth century Celtic grave in Bohemia. Many finely worked Celtic bronze helmets have been discovered.

Celtic Weapons

The Celtic warrior ready for battle wore a long sword hanging from an iron or bronze chain on his right side (vs. the shorter stabbing sword of the Romans). Strabo wrote that the Celtic soldier also typically carried spears or lances, and mentioned a separate javelin-like weapon called a *madaris*. He said that slings and bows were used but that they were not considered important weapons.

Celtic fighting men also carried a large shield made of wood or leather, sometimes part bronze, which covered the body from the knees to the shoulders. Many Celtic aristocrats rode chariots into battle. Some soldiers were designated the task of blowing elaborate war trumpets. These made a harsh sound, Diodorus observed, "which suits the tumult of war."

Battle Of Telamon

The acquaintanceship between the ancient Celts and Romans endured for eight centuries. As with other peoples, the milestones marking the important dates of their common history are mostly of invasions, wars and battles. As with other nations, before and since, the impact of what Celts did (or had done to them) in war was what made history. During the third and second centuries B.C. the Celts continued to value chivalry and personal heroism; ideally warrior against warrior in single, hand-to-hand combat, even as their armies watched. The Celts may even have then considered it unmanly for a Celtic nobleman to kill an enemy from afar with such a weapon as a bow and arrow, while the Romans were closer to thinking of war in modern terms, using any available technique; the newer and more surprising the better.

In 225 B.C. the battle of Telamon (in Italy's Tuscany) marked the beginning of the Celts' decline in continental Europe. Although at first successful when they killed a Roman consul, the Celts were trapped at Telamon between two Roman armies and lost twenty-five thousand men. Polybius wrote that "the numbers who took part and perished in the battle is second to no war in history."

It was the beginning of the end of Celtic dominance in Italy, just as it represented the stirrings of a burgeoning Roman Republic on its way to becoming an empire. The definitive encounter in continental Europe between Romans and Celts, however, would not occur for another 173 years—in France. In the meantime there would be countless other encounters between Celts and Romans in various countries.

Hannibal And His Celtic Allies

The Second "Punic" War (218-201 B.C.) between Rome and the north African city-state of Carthage was one of the great struggles in history. The Carthaginian general Hannibal is famous for marching his elephant-equipped army from Spain into France, crossing the snowbound Alps, and dramatically descending into Italy from the north to attack the Romans. It is not generally known that along the way Hannibal's army was augmented by Celts from Gaul, without whose knowledge it could not have found its way across the snowy Alps of winter. Reaching northern Italy's Po Valley, Hannibal was joined by thousands of Celtic allies who were settled there.

Roman Army Defeated

In 217 B.C. Hannibal and his Celtic allies defeated the main Roman army at Italy's Lake Trasimeno. From there he went on to plunder Italy at will, defying the Romans to stop him. But even with the Celts on his side, he never tried to take Rome itself. Learning from experience, the Romans had built a new city wall and considerably strengthened its defense system since the Celts sacked it 183 years earlier.

Romans Seek Protection From "The Great Mother"

In the Rome of 205 B.C. a hail of pebbles from the sky, probably from Mount Vesuvius, inspired a religious belief that Hannibal and perhaps even the Celts would leave Italy if the Great Mother was brought to Rome from the Greek city of Pergamum. The deity known as The Great Mother, originally Asiatic, was known and accepted by the Greeks and Romans as Cybele. As guardian of cities and nations she was entrusted with the general welfare of the people, and was represented as either riding a chariot drawn by two lions or sitting on a throne flanked by two lions.

Cybele was then worshipped in the form of a hallowed, black stone (actually a meteorite) in the Greek kingdom of Pergamum in Turkey. There King Attalus I (the same one who made the famed nude Gaesatae statues) diplomatically chose to placate the demanding and ever more powerful Romans and released the stone to them. This otherwise nondescript piece of rock arrived in Italy by sea, somehow being thought of as The Great Mother herself. The renowned general, Scipio (who would later defeat Hannibal in Africa), respectfully boarded the ship to receive her. The stone was then proudly carried through the streets of Rome by that city's noblest matrons and placed reverently in the temple of Victory. As forecast, Hannibal left Italy two years later in 203 B.C. never to return. The Celts stayed on.

In 153 B.C. Romans in Spain regretted using elephants in their attack against the Celtic hillfort of *Numantia.* From high on the fort walls the Celtic defenders dropped a rock onto the head of one of the attacking elephants which drove it crazy with anger. Trumpeting furiously the great beast turned against its own side, trampling and gouging and panicking the other elephants into a complete Roman rout.

One Roman commander in Spain, Titus Didius, set about defeating some Celts without elephants. He invited the entire population of the local Celtic community inside his stockade on the pretense of a proposal to apportion local land. Didius then closed the gates and had his soldiers slaughter the assembled families who were his unarmed guests. The Greek writer of Roman history, Appian, wrote in disgust that for his deed "Didius was actually honoured with a triumph."

The Third (and last) Punic War (149-146 B.C.) was, like the first two, started by deliberate Roman aggression. But this time the Carthaginians did not have the help of the Celts. At the end of the war Rome razed the city of Carthage, sold its surviving inhabitants into slavery, and ploughed up the site of the city itself (and, so the story goes, seeded the soil with salt).

One hundred years later, Cicero wrote of his disgust at the staging of barbaric entertainment in Rome, which included the slaughter of eighteen elephants. It was perhaps a symbolic act of revenge for the humiliating time when the elephant-equipped Hannibal and his Celtic allies terrified Rome and marched unchallenged throughout much of Italy.

The 2134-Year Wait

A unique footnote to the Carthage-Rome (Punic) wars occurred in 1988 A.D. It was only then that the mayors of the modern cities of Carthage and Rome finally signed a treaty of "friendship and cooperation" officially ending the hostilities that began between them 2252 years earlier—in 264 B.C. It had taken more than two thousand years but, as the *Times of London* put it, "officialdom in Rome never moved fast."

Back at the end of the second century B.C., however, Rome was then keeping a wary eye on the Celts who had not only founded Milan and farmed in what later would become known as northern "Italy" (as they had done for centuries), but had dared to take sides with Hannibal and his elephants. It was, however, another Celtic-speaking people who took the Romans by surprise.

7

End of the Continental Celts

Celts Defeat Roman Armies

In 106 B.C. the Celts known as the *Volcae Tectosages* defeated the Roman army of Cassius Longinus and forced his surviving legionaries to demonstrate their subservience by having them literally march under the yoke. At about the same time the Celtic-speaking *Cimbri* entered Italy and decimated several Roman armies. But the Cimbri were the last people to seriously threaten the Romans within the borders of Italy for hundreds of years to come.

The Romans' repeated confrontations with the Celts led to an extensive reorganization of the Roman army in 104 B.C. by a general named Caius Marius. It was he who made it into the deadly fighting machine that Julius Caesar would later use against other peoples in much of the known world—including the last of the independent Celts in continental Europe.

Marius' innovations were most effective. In 101 B.C. he defeated the Cimbri in a battle near Milan. The vast and fertile territory south of the Alps occupied by the Celts since the fourth century B.C. was then permanently annexed by Rome to become the northern part of a country that would be known as Italy. Five hundred years would pass before Italy was invaded and the Roman army again defeated—this time not by the Celts, but by the Germans.

How The Roman Army Was Reorganized

The most important step Caius Marius took in changing the Roman army was to make it a professional one of long-service soldiers. This replaced the traditional citizen army composed of Latin farmers recruited in emergencies. At the same time Marius saw to it that officers were chosen for their professionalism and not for their social position.

The creation of a standing army offered to both educated and peasant Roman citizens an organized, professional career, complete with pride in an institution of national importance, regular pay (unlike the citizen army), free food, accommodation, medical services, a chance to see the world, endless opportunities to obtain loot, and substantial cash payments from compulsory army savings accounts on retirement. Enlistment was from 16-20 years. The intent of the Roman system of military training, Vegetius later wrote, was to make warfare "not a dread, but a delight."

Marius did away with the phalanx method of battle in which the Romans charged en masse, counting on this tactic to destroy or at least scatter the enemy. Instead he developed the strategy of attacking by sections, each with its own lethal speciality, and under the calculating command of a professional career officer whose future in Rome depended on winning on the battlefield against people like the Celts or the Germans. The relatively short, double-edged sword developed by the Spanish Celts was adopted by the Romans. They correctly believed that a stabbing wound to the body with this easily maneuvered weapon was more often fatal than a slashing wound from an longer sword that was likely to be blocked by bones from reaching a vital organ.

Eagle Power Symbol

Finally Marius created an entirely new concept, the *Aquila* or eagle standard as a visible symbol of unity for the Roman legions to rally around. To lose it was a disgrace.

Paintings of war scenes in later centuries frequently portray heroic standard-bearers who (whether victorious, threatened, or dying) can be seen steadfastly grasping the regimental colors or national flag. Whatever its design, the concept of these more recent standards may have originated in the Roman Silver Eagle or Aquila.

The Silver Eagle standard, like a living person, had an annual birthday celebrated with pomp and ceremony. It would witness numerous of battles and the violent deaths of thousands, many of them Celts.

The Three-Way Crunch

For seven centuries, from about 750-50 B.C., the various branches of the Celtic people formed a nation of great power and influence, for a time collectively holding control over much of Europe, even to having sacked Rome and invaded Greece. But the middle of the first century B.C. would see the end of the Celtic nation in mainland Europe. Pressured by Germanic tribes expanding from the north, by the Dacians spreading from the east, and by Rome from the south, most independent Celts in continental Europe by 60 B.C. were confined to what is now Switzerland, France, Belgium, and the islands of Britain and Ireland. Only encounters between Romans and Celts, however, were historically documented—many of them by Julius Caesar who wrote much of his own history.

In 58 B.C., Caesar was an aspiring politician—a proconsul—who still had a long way to go before becoming dictator of Rome. Many of the important events in his career occurred after he was made militarily responsible for the Celtic-inhabited areas south and north of the Alps (Cisalpine and Transalpine Gaul). It was in the political and economic interests of Rome, as it was for Caesar himself, to keep his expensive horde of paid, professional soldiers gainfully employed—and he did. One of his first objectives in achieving this was to seek out and destroy a large but relatively defenseless and peaceful group of Celtic farmers and their families.

The Helvetii Massacre

In 60 B.C. the Helvetii Celts, living in what is now Switzerland, began preparations to migrate from their cramped lands between the mountains to wider pastures in Gaul/France, which had by then become the heartland of the Celtic people. An additional incentive was to move away from the constant threat of aggressive German neighbors. The Helvetii spent two years getting ready for the move. Preparations included the production of enough surplus crops for two seasons and building hundreds of wagons. Writing in Greek, detailed lists were made of all able-bodied men, old men, women and children. They finally set out in 58 B.C. Before leaving they burned their fortified settlements, villages and farming homesteads so that they would not be tempted to return.

Caesar heard of the Helvetii migration and decided to destroy it. Declaring these Celtic farmers an enemy of Rome and annihilating them was one way of receiving popular and political approval and getting his name better known back home. Neither the Celts nor the Romans could have known that there would one day be a Switzerland, or that it would be proudly given the official "poetic" name of Helvetia in honour of its Helvetii Celtic heritage.

Commanding several legions of well equipped and highly skilled professional troops, Caesar attacked the Helvetii Celtic farmers and their families, savagely slaughtering six thousand of them. Many of the survivors—about a third of the original migration—struggled back to the scorched land in Switzerland they had never expected to see again.

Having disposed of the Helvetii Celts, Caesar's next move would be to "pacify" Celtic Gaul where he planned for a victory he needed to advance his ambition for a political career in Rome. He knew that this action would at the same time provide him with the opportunity to acquire great numbers of slaves which would gain him considerable personal wealth. What he could not have known was that, even with his thousands of deadly soldiers, it would take him eight years to subdue the Gaulish Celts. His approach to warfare, while acceptable for his time, would not be considered efficient today.

For Caesar, summer and its agreeable weather was the fashionable season for his military campaigns against the Celts from 58 to 49 B.C. Ideally, he went south to spend the winters in Rome, leaving his army in winter quarters in Gaul under a second-in-command until campaigning began again in the pleasant weather of spring. From Caesar's perspective, he made the most of the eight years he spent battling the Celts in Gaul, considered by the Romans back home to be an exotic but dangerous place. He personally wrote the only detailed, firsthand account of his relentless exploits against the Celts, a people who had never been forgiven by the Romans for sacking and occupying their city more than three centuries earlier—even if it was in retaliation to the unethical murder by a Roman envoy of a Celtic chief in Etruria. For Caesar, being "Savior of Rome" meant being Rome's executive warlord in Gaul with life and death privileges over its population. Not only would no questions be asked if in a single day he killed hundreds of Celtic men, women and children, he was likely, since he wrote his own reports, to be credited with a triumph by Rome.

By his own count, Caesar killed 1,192,000 men, women and children in eight years as he "pacified" Celtic Gaul. (In contrast, two thousand years later, World War II cost Italy 262,000 military and 93,000 civilian lives). Yet two thousand years later he is best remembered for his genius than for the vast numbers of people he slaughtered.

Caesar The Man

Caesar's contemporary, Asinius Pollio—literary critic, consul, and founder of Rome's public library—accused Caesar of accepting at face value the accounts of officers in the field. He also actually accused Caesar of distorting events to his credit. Although naturally biased and at times self-serving, Caesar's *Gallic War* (seven books) is, however, among the finest examples of concise Latin of his time. They are considered classic military documents and are greatly valued for their information on his eight-year war with the Celts. No matter that they incorporated some fanciful material, including his report on a creature with one horn—a unicorn—he claimed lived in the Hercynian Forest.

Julius Caesar was born in Rome in July, 102 B.C. of a noble family, and claimed actual descent from the goddess Venus. His birth was difficult, with a surgeon introducing him into the world through an incision cut in his mother's abdomen, an operation that would henceforth bear his name—Caesarean section.

At age 14 Caesar was made a priest of the sacred College of Jupiter through the influence of his powerful uncle Caius Marius. Besides unwittingly giving his name to an unnatural, non-vaginal method of birth, Julius Caesar also gave one of his names to the month of July.

The study of Caesar by Plutarch (the most famous source for Caesar, and the one used by Shakespeare) is unflattering, calling him a man corrupted by power, degenerating by degrees into a tyrant and a monster. Suetonius, his earliest biographer, however, provides personal details indicating that he was quite human:

> Caesar is said to have been tall, fair, and well-built, with a rather broad face and keen, dark brown eyes...He was something of a dandy, always keeping his head carefully trimmed and shaved; and has been accused of having certain other hairy parts of his body depilated with tweezers. His baldness was a disfigurement which his enemies harped upon, much to his exasperation; but he used to comb the thin strands of hair forward from his poll, and of all the honours voted him by the Senate and people, none pleased him so much as the privilege of wearing a laurel wreath on all occasions—he constantly took advantage of it.

It was reported that Caesar suffered epileptic seizures which he tried to keep secret.

Caesar The Military Genius

Much has been said for and against Julius Caesar. Admirers among his fellow Romans saw him as the defender of the rights of the (Roman) people. Others saw him as an ambitious demagogue who forced his way to dictatorial power. Some modern scholars say he was a genius. All agree that he was one of the greatest generals of all time.

A skillful exponent of the divide-and-rule method, Caesar was ever ready to take advantage of feuds among the hundreds of independent Celtic rulers in Gaul, some of whom fought on his side against other Celts if the feud ran deep enough. Indeed some Celts provided the best cavalry that ever fought for Caesar in Gaul. If the Celts had been a unified people, Caesar probably would never have defeated them to become a hero to Rome—and the political face of Europe might have been different today.

In 54 B.C. Caesar was thus winning his Gallic "War" at least in part because the structure of the Celtic nation allowed him to fight the Gauls tribe by tribe. It was a case of his numerous legions, each comprising thousands of professional soldiers, against whatever volunteer "army" each chieftain or king could muster from his farmer subjects in the event of predatory Romans approaching his territory. In this respect many of the military "achievements" claimed by Caesar were easily won, if not outrightly hypocritical. In the process of killing 1,192,000 men, women and children in Gaul, the Roman legions took more than eight hundred "towns." To the populace of Rome, Caesar's exploits in exotic places were making him the hero he had set out to be. Such recognition was a calculated part of his long-term political plans.

The Last Chance

To retain their independence and their country, the Celts all across Gaul desperately needed to come together under one leader. They needed someone with the ability to unite their nation against the invasion of Caesar's single-minded killing machine that was systematically working its destructive way through their country like a hungry worm in an apple. It would have to be a leader who would organize

Gaul's traditionally independent tribal groups into a coordinated, single army.

Towards the end, some Celtic rulers did see beyond their tradition of tribal independence and tried to act on a concept of national Celtic unity. But, with a destructive Caesar already in their midst, these individuals began their various attempts at collective retaliation too late. Celtic "soldiers" in Gaul were farmers first and warriors only in emergencies, with each man owing allegiance to his local chief or king rather than to a national cause.

CELTIC HEROES 54-52 B.C.

Dumnorix was one of the Celtic leaders in France who challenged the territorial advances of Rome into his homeland. A nobleman of the *Aedui* Celts in Gaul, he became known to Caesar for his patriotic efforts to rally both his own people and other Celtic tribes against the invading Romans. While being killed later on Caesar's instructions, he cried repeatedly, "I am a free man in a free state."

King Ambiorix of the *Eburones* (one of the Celtic tribes that inhabited present-day Belgium) attacked and defeated a local Roman garrison planted in his territory. Encouraged with this success, Ambiorix organized two other Celtic tribes to join him in attacking yet another Roman garrison.

Constructing Roman-type scaling towers and grappling hooks, they showered the thatched roofs of the Roman encampment with blazing darts which started a serious fire. Caesar himself arrived with a relieving army and saved the garrison, but the myth of Roman invincibility had been exposed.

A Roman army was sent to capture Ambiorix, but without success. A vengeful Caesar, however, killed many of the people in Ambiorix's kingdom while destroying every village and farm and all the crops and animals he could find. Of the people who escaped being killed, Caesar wrote with satisfaction, "it seemed certain that they must die of starvation."

At another time and place in Gaul, with the approach of rampaging Roman legions, forty thousand Celtic farmers and their families took refuge in the fortified Celtic town of Avaricum. But after twenty-seven days of siege the Romans finally forced their way in and slaughtered all the men, women and children they could find. The hardworking Celtic farmers had stored a large quantity of grain in Avaricum. Having themselves run out of food, the Romans had to take Avaricum or starve.

Acco was another Celtic leader who rebelled against Rome. He led a combined but unsuccessful revolt of the *Senones* and the *Carnutes* against the Roman presence in his country. He was punished by being flogged and put to death in a display to entertain Roman troops. Caesar later captured and killed his equally rebellious successor, Guturatos, and sent his decapitated head around Gaul as a warning. Guturatos and Acco made it into the history books, but they are not so well known as a fellow Celtic patriot with whose violent death they would have much in common.

Vercingetorix

A Celtic chief named *Vercingetorix* decimated a Roman army when it attempted to take the Celtic town of Gergovia. In this battle, Caesar admitted losing seven hundred men, including forty-six of his centurions, the "backbone" of the Roman fighting machine. After seven years of Caesar's depredations the victory was a great boost to Celtic resistance. But Caesar moved quickly to reestablish his military superiority so that he could take revenge on this Celtic leader, Vercingetorix, who had so ably defeated him at Gergovia.

Vercingetorix, a powerful personality, was described as young, handsome, and exceedingly tall. As chief of the Celtic *Arverni* he embarked on a mission to fight the Romans by unifying the Celtic tribes as a single force—what Caesar feared most. Ignoring petty rivalries, Vercingetorix used his victory at Gergovia to gather recruits from neighboring tribes. As determined and ruthless as Caesar, he imposed a strict discipline, punishing with death those who did not cooperate with his *national* cause. He adopted a "scorched-earth" policy, burning Celtic towns and crops to prevent Caesar's troops from living off the land. He applied guerrilla warfare to cut off the Romans' supplies.

Caesar was alarmed and reinforced his cavalry with German horsemen. As supreme commander of Roman forces in Gaul he joined his own army with that of one of his generals, Labienus, and set out to *get* Vercingetorix at any cost. After seven years of war he needed a clear-cut victory over this Celtic chieftain, or return to Rome in disgrace, his lofty political ambitions ruined.

ALESIA: THE FINAL CHALLENGE

In 52 B.C. Vercingetorix established his headquarters in the fortified town of Alesia where he stockpiled enough food to last twenty thousand men for thirty days. But he had not counted on the absolute determination and seemingly unlimited resources of Caesar to destroy him.

Caesar surrounded the hill of Alesia with his legions, thousands of men in each, including companies of engineers—and began to construct the most elaborate siege works of his entire career. It was clear that these siege works were intended to let no one escape from the hill.

Water was deflected from two streams to form a moat twenty feet wide. Above this was built a rampart and palisades fourteen kilometers long with turrets set at eighty-foot intervals. Other items included what Caesar called *stimuli*—camouflaged iron barbs set in the ground, along with rows of pits covered with brush and lined at the bottom with sharpened stakes. Then, in case of attack from the surrounding countryside, the Romans built a second defense facing outward that was twenty-two kilometers long.

Alesia's food ran out in the next few weeks as many Celts died in discovering the impregnability of what the Romans built around the bottom of the hill.

The Sacrifice

With his people dying of starvation, Vercingetorix accepted responsibility for the failed revolt. He called together his chieftains and told them: "I did not undertake the war for private ends, but in the cause of national liberty. And since I must now accept my fate, I place myself at your disposal. Make amends to the Romans by killing me or surrender me alive as you think best." (Recorded from witnesses by Caesar himself).

The chieftains did not kill Vercingetorix, but they too remembered the slaughter at Avaricum. The gates were opened and Vercingetorix left Alesia for his fateful meeting with the Romans massed below.

The final scene at Alesia is dramatic. Riding tall and proud on his caparisoned horse, and wearing the finest Celtic-made silver and enameled armor, Vercingetorix descends the hill alone and slowly makes a ritual sunwise circle around the dais where Caesar sits surrounded by his generals and the standards of his legions. Dismounting, he throws aside his weapons and silently awaits his conqueror's pleasure.

Caesar's pleasure is to send Vercingetorix in chains to Rome where he is dragged through the streets in triumph. The senate, in gratitude for Caesar's victory, declares a twenty-day public thanksgiving. Six years later, in 45 B.C., the year he is named Dictator of Rome for life, Caesar proudly exhibits Vercingetorix in the Forum and then has him strangled.

Alesia Today

Two thousand years later, near the modern city of Dijon, the hill of Alesia (Mont Auxois) is still there for all to see. On a small part of it sits the medieval village of Alise Sainte Reine (Alesia). Sections of Caesar's complex and formidable siege works are there too, carefully reconstructed full-size in every detail. The French have erected an imposing statue of their noble ancestor, Vercingetorix. At the National Museum of Antiquities at St. Germain en Laye there are models of the various man-killing traps set by the Romans at the foot of the hill.

Fate Of The Continental Celts

The Celts remained as the indigenous population of Gaul/France (the Celtic *Parisii* giving their name to Paris). But never again would they seriously challenge the might of Rome. Future military glory would be achieved only as auxiliaries fighting for Roman armies. Celtic settlements in France became Romanized market towns, and the Celtic language evolved into French. The Academie Francaise acknowledges the presence of about five hundred Celtic words in modern French, with the possibility of there being many more. The ancient Celts counted in twenties. The rural French people of today still buy things by twenties—by the score. "Four twenties" is how they say "eighty" in modern French—and in the surviving Celtic or Gaelic language in Ireland.

Centuries later, the Romanized Celts would mix with invading German Franks, just as the Celts in Italy, Switzerland, Germany and elsewhere would blend with others in forming new nations. The Franks gave their name to France, but today's French people have much Celtic blood flowing in their veins.

After the capture of Vercingetorix in 52 B.C. the only remaining free and independent Celts were in Britain and Ireland.

Caesar's Invasions Of Britain

Julius Caesar had no plan to create a permanent Roman settlement on the occasion of his first invasion of the Celtic island of Britain in 55 B.C. He intended this visit only as a reconnaissance expedition and a show of force toward the island Celts who freely traded, aided, and fraternized with their fellow Celts (and his enemies) in Gaul. Above all, he hoped that his journey to the very edge of the world would impress Rome with his daring—which it did. He crossed the English Channel on August 24, 55 B.C., taking two legions with him—about ten thousand men, and leaving four legions to take care of the Celts in Gaul until he returned.

The Roman soldiers invading Britain were surprised to find its inhabitants, the Celtic Britons, riding two-horse chariots into battle, a mode of warfare no longer used on the continent and which must have been daunting to encounter.

Probably most unnerving to the Romans, however, was the reported custom of collecting enemy heads in battle—especially when they were Roman heads.

Yet head hunting was not unknown in Rome itself. When Caesar's contemporary, the classical writer Cicero, expressed a political difference with his fellow Romans, Anthony and Octavius, he was hunted through the streets of Rome like an animal and killed; his head and right hand cut off and put on public display in the Forum. A century later, in 69 A.D., the Roman emperor Galba and many of his supporters would have their heads hacked off and displayed on poles in Rome alongside the standards of the Roman legion.

Caesar's first invasion of Britain lasted for only a few weeks and achieved nothing militarily, except for some skirmishes with southern Celtic groups. To take care of his expenses, he brought back slaves from Britain. Ironically, he transported his invasion force—and his slaves—on ships built by Brittany's seafaring Celts, the *Veneti*. These were substantial ships 140 to 150 feet long with a beam of 16 feet.

Celtic Shipbuilders, First Century B.C.

The Celtic Veneti's territory, *Armorica*, lay in France's present-day Brittany, which juts into the storm-prone Atlantic. Their coastal capital, Vannes, is still there today, populated by the descendants of the Veneti Celts. Strabo described the seaworthy Veneti-built ships used by Caesar in his invasion of Britain:

> "The timber of their boats was thick, their sails made of leather, owing to the force of the (Atlantic) winds.... They make their boats with broad bottoms and high sterns and prows, on account of the ebb-tides. The material is oak...and therefore they do not joint their

> planks closely, but leave openings which they stop with seaweed, so that when the boats are in dock the wood may not dry up for lack of moisture, the seaweed being naturally rather moist, while the oak is dry and without fat."

Caesar wrote admiringly of these Celtic seafarers:

> "The Veneti are the most powerful tribe on the Brittany coast. They have the largest fleet of ships, in which they traffic with Britain...and as the coast lies exposed to the violence of the open sea and has but few harbors, which the Veneti control, they compel nearly all who sail the waters to pay toll."

Back in Rome, Caesar was greeted with great enthusiasm after his first overseas adventure. The senate proposed a period of thanksgiving for his having successfully faced the unknown hazards of Britain (something the Celts had done centuries earlier). For his part, Caesar had already planned to again invade Britain the following year. This time he would have twenty-eight war galleys and six hundred transport ships to carry three times more men than on his first invasion. He was not looking for homesteading land. If Britain had been an uninhabited island, he and his successors in Rome would not have found it so appealing. There would have been no glory and no commercial profit in conquering an island devoid of people.

Caesar's second invasion of Celtic Britain, in 54 B.C., was intended to establish a permanent Roman presence on the island. But once again he was confused in finding himself facing a complex political situation represented by the numerous independent Celtic kingdoms, some of which did not take kindly to his belligerent intrusion. As on his first visit, he saw very little of Britain or its people. During a "campaign" of less than three (traditionally summer) months on the island, he dutifully fought battles, accumulated commercially valuable slaves, and signed a treaty with the British Celts known as the *Trinovantes*. In autumn he sailed with his fleet from Britain never to return.

After defeating the Celts in France and having invaded Celtic Britain, Caesar went on to defeat Ptolemy, King of Egypt, establish Cleopatra as queen on the throne of Egypt, spend time in her bed, father a son (named Caesarion), and finally, in 44 B.C., die from twenty-three stab wounds inflicted by his fellow Romans, as he presided over the senate in Rome. He was deified by the Romans after his death.

Ninety-seven years passed before men from the boot-shaped Italian peninsula in the warm Mediterranean would again attempt to turn the Celtic island of Britannia into a Roman province.

8

ISLANDS AT THE END OF THE EARTH

Women As Gods

The ancient Celts were exceptional in their preference for goddesses over gods. Yet this may not be surprising in a people who had female rulers, invented chivalry, and were far ahead of their time in having equal rights for men and women. While the Romans created a goddess of sewers (*Cloacina*), the Celts had goddesses for things they revered, such as the forest, and horses—and even war. While the Romans made Mars their god of war, the Celts had a female deity for theirs.

Celtic goddesses were frequently associated with healing powers, others with fertility and bounty. Each was in some way a reflection of an earth-mother goddess. Even the sometimes fierce *Mórrígan*, the "great queen" and goddess of war in Irish mythology, was also essentially a mother-goddess of fertility.

Julius Caesar is one of many classical writers who provides contemporary—if not always firsthand—written accounts of the ancient Celts. In one of his more unusual entries he claims to have found some Celtic women possessing several husbands; a practice that would never have been allowed in patriarchal Rome. "The man who first married the woman," he noted, "is recognized as the father to the children of such a marriage." While Caesar may or may not have witnessed polyandry among the Celts, such a practice would probably have been documented by others if it was common. The

Greek and Roman writers liked to enliven their works with accounts of what they perceived as licentious behavior among the Celts.

Often, however, items written by the classical writers were supportive of the Celts. Dio Cassius, for example, presented a rare Celtic point of view when he quoted the reply of a Celtic wife to a jeering accusation of promiscuity from a Roman matron:

> "We fulfill the demands of nature in a much better way than do you Roman women," the Celtic lady retorted disdainfully, "for we consort openly with the best men, whereas you let yourselves be debauched in secret by the vilest."

Some classical writers, such as Strabo, gave their opinion on the more earthy qualities of Celtic women. After discussing the impressive size of various Celtic populations, he admiringly mentions "the excellence of their women in bearing and rearing children." This, he wrote sagely, compelled the men to devote themselves to food production. No part of the Celtic land, he added, "was unworked except for swamps and thickets." It can be assumed that he would have included the Celtic women of Britain in this general description.

Daily Life Of The Celts

There are many classical references to the fastidious habits of the early Celts who washed themselves with soap—which the classical historian Diodorus Siculus credits the Celts with inventing. The Celts also used oils and sweet herbs to anoint their bodies. Numerous Celtic-made razors and combs and beautifully made bronze mirrors have been found, the best known example being the *Desborough Mirror* found in England. Warriors traditionally insisted on wearing a clean

The engraved back of the two-thousand-year-old, Celtic-made, bronze Desborough Mirror. Both a work of art and a symbol of metallic technology from Celtic Britain. Photo by James P. Blair, ©1977 National Geographic Society.

tunic before going into battle. The Celts, however, were equally known for their food preferences, and their ability and methods of satisfying them.

The "sport" of fox hunting by "riding to hound" in today's Britain and Ireland originated with the Celtic aristocracy and their love for boar and deer hunting from horseback, accompanied by their "clever" hunting dogs (the breeding of which the Celts considered an art). A dramatic 2,100-year-old Celtic bronze tableau shows a spear-armed Celtic nobleman on his galloping horse, accompanied by his hound, in pursuit of a boar.

Traditional food for the Celts in Britain and Ireland included boiled pork, roast beef, bread, game and fish; along with cheese, curds, milk and butter, mead, beer, and imported wine for the wealthy. Ale was the common brew and was made from barley, sometimes from rye or oats. Having all or most of these at the same time indicated a feast or banquet. At the banquets of a chief, king, or queen, minstrels played lyres and sang of love and bravery—or satirized any of the nobility present for more spontaneous, original entertainment.

Meat was boiled or, according to Athenaeus, "roasted on charcoal or on spits." Meat was preserved in salt for winter use. A favorite Celtic dish was baked salmon with honey and herbs. Athenaeus said that fish was also baked with salt, vinegar and cumin. A less exotic-sounding staple was porridge. The Irish sagas mention the eating of edible seaweed such as *carrageen* which is still eaten in Ireland and Scotland in modern times. The Welsh use seaweed in making *laver* bread. The Celts did not invent whisky until the twelfth century when the still was invented. The Irish word "whiskey" (Scottish "whisky") is an anglicization of Celtic words meaning "water of life."

A "cult" wagon from second-century B.C. *Spain portraying a Celtic horseman and his dog hunting a wild boar.*
Photo from Cluny Museum/R.M.N., *Paris, France.*

Battersea Shield. A Celtic work of art in enameled bronze recovered from England's River Thames in 1855. Now in the British Museum. Photo by James P. Blair. © National Geographic Society.

The Celts, whose own "heroic" society had invented the concept of the noble knight (to be perpetuated and immortalized by the legendary Celtic King Arthur), were aware of a generous diet's consequences. They considered it a disgrace for a man to become fat and flabby. Strabo wrote of the Celts he knew: "The Celtic men try not to become stout and fat-bellied, and any young man who exceeds the standard length of the girdle is fined." Strabo leaves his readers wondering who would impose or collect the fine.

Clothing

The Romans invading Britain found its Celtic inhabitants looking, living, and dressing much the same as the Celts of Gaul (and much the same as those in Ireland, had they known of their existence). Caesar mentioned the traffic between the two regions—Gaul and Britain. After the Roman legionaries had been in Britain for some time in the chilly northern climate, they abandoned their skirt-like toga and adopted the Celtic trousers called *bracae*. Bracae would eventually be corrupted to breeches as the word for trousers in English. In a unisex fashion, bracae were also sometimes worn by women, although they more commonly wore a tight-waisted skirt (bell-shaped in some Celtic regions). Leather shoes and sandals were worn by both sexes.

Both men and women wore belted tunics reaching either to the hips or to the knees. Over this was worn a cloak, again by both men and women, fastened with a brooch as fancy as the wearer could afford—sometimes gold or silver. The women sometimes attached little tinkling bells to theirs. Cloaks could be especially fancy, and frequently indicated social status and rank. Ancient texts refer to the cloaks of Irish kings as being "five-folded." Dio Cassius wrote that Queen Boudicca "wore a great twisted golden necklace, and a tunic of many colors over which was a thick cloak, fastened by a brooch." In her speeding chariot she must have presented a spectacular sight to the foot-slogging Roman soldiers.

Brilliantly dyed, hooded wool cloaks made by Celts in Gaul and Britain became internationally famous. These garments were heavily taxed and worn only by the wealthy in Rome. There they continued to be highly valued for centuries, even after the collapse of the Roman Empire. Some Celtic cloth merchants became wealthy enough from the art of weaving to build fancy mausoleums for themselves.

Other items imported from Celtic Britain to Rome, according to Strabo, included corn, livestock, metals, leather, slaves and "clever" hunting dogs. Caesar wrote that he saw the Celts in Britain with large herds of cattle and flocks of sheep. Celts at that time in Britain and Ireland in part measured their wealth in livestock.

Exquisitely made horse harnesses and metal chariot fittings were produced by the Celts mainly for their own use. A classical historian reported seeing a Celtic (probably ceremonial) war chariot entirely covered in silver.

Items imported by the Britons included ivory, jewelry, bronze-fitted furniture, silver tableware, and wine. From the second century B.C., various Celtic kingdoms in Britain minted their own coins of gold or silver. While some of these showed chariots, most had heads on one side, while on the other side were various animals that included horses, boars, lions, bears and eagles. Modern Irish coins have a harp on one side, and animals currently found in Ireland on the other.

Hair Styles

Caesar described Briton men as having long hair with shaven faces but with moustaches. The women liked to wear their hair long, and it is thought that their beauty was much judged by the condition and color of their tresses. Often their hair was braided into two or three pigtails which were then brought together with combs or secured with gold or silver ornamental clips. Although sources vary, they generally indicate that the typical appearance of early Celtic society was that of tall, physically powerful men and women with fair or reddish hair, grey or blue eyes, light skins and fresh complexions.

Yet not all ancient Celts were blond or reddish-headed (any more than all Celts are today). In 38 A.D., when the emperor Caligula planned to parade a group of Celtic captives through the streets of Rome, he ordered the hair of the darker prisoners to be dyed an exotic red so that the Latin people would have no doubt that they were seeing real Celts.

Diodorus Siculus inexplicably wrote of Celtic women:

> "Their children are born, for the most part, with grey hair, but as they advance in age they are assimilated to the hair color of their parents."

Presented by Diodorus as fact, this may well have been a story told by a mischievous, straight-faced Celt and passed on, perhaps years later, to a gullible Diodorus who did not see the joke. Otherwise it is one of the more unusual fantasies created by invariably biased, often hostile outsiders writing of the Celts. It is tempting to think that Diodorus would have relished the opportunity to write his "reports" for a modern tabloid.

Games And Sports

The field game of hurley, also known as hurling, was popular in pre-Roman Britain. (In Ireland it still is). Played by opposing teams using sticks and a ball, it is not unlike hockey. Celtic mythology tells of the Irish King Conchobar dividing his day into three parts and choosing to spend the first third of it watching the youths playing games and hurling, a story indicating that competitive games were an important social activity, especially among the sons of the nobility. The story goes on to say the king would spend the second part of his day playing the board games of *brandub* and *fidchell*.

Known and played by the Welsh as *gwyddbwyll*, fidchell means "wooden wisdom." With two opposing sets of figures on the board, it was not unlike chess. In the Irish story, *The Wooing of Etain*, a game is played lasting for several days between the god *Midir* (disguised as an ordinary mortal), and *Eochaid Airem*, King of Ireland. They use a "chess" board and pieces made of silver and gold. The stakes are the king's lovely wife, *Etain* (who is really a goddess). Midir, more powerful than a mere king, wins. He and Etain are last seen flying over Tara metamorphosed as beautiful swans.

Being a king, the third part of Conchobar's day was spent with others consuming food and drink and being entertained by minstrels and musicians.

Bonding By Fosterage

Aristocratic Celtic society in Ireland and Britain practiced the custom of *fosterage* whereby noble families of lesser rank would send their sons and daughters to be reared in the households of kings and chiefs and other higher-ranking families where they would be taught the ways of the nobility. This would include sewing and embroidering for the girls and more "manly" pursuits for the boys such as horse riding, hunting, sword fighting, and, in quieter moments, the playing of fidchell and brandub.

Inherent in the fostering system was the control it provided the chiefs over the noble families of the children in their care. Boys were eventually returned to their parents at about 17 years, the girls at about 14 (or at puberty when they were considered marriageable). Close lifelong bonds often developed between children fostered in the same home.

Although they stayed longer with their foster families, boys were considered less expensive than girls to educate because they were less trouble to raise and also more likely to help pay their way by providing service. The aristocratic Celts' high regard for women was reflected in their view that girls were more expensive to raise than boys because, being more fastidious, they required more attendants.

The Celtic Homestead

The ancient Celts built two kinds of structures—the domestic dwelling (usually a farmhouse), and the fortified "town" or *oppida*. In Britain and Ireland most Celtic families lived on individual farms. Strabo provided a description of the Belgae dwellings which would apply to much of Britain and Ireland: "Their houses are large and circular, built of planks and wickerwork, the roof being a dome of heavy thatch." In each house a great metal cauldron was suspended on an iron chain from a crossbeam over the central fire, the smoke escaping through a hole at the top of the conical roof. Typically fifty feet in diameter, these large houses incorporated partitioned areas that served as rooms. In some areas of Britain and Ireland the houses were rectangular, and two- and three-storied. The houses of noblemen were substantial and set in their own fortified compounds with other buildings for servants and agricultural needs.

Stone Dwellings

Where wood was scarce, as in parts of Scotland, Celtic dwellings were made of stone. The largest of these are called *brochs* and date from the second century B.C. and possibly earlier. An example that is still standing partially intact can be seen at Clickhimin, Scotland. Reaching over forty feet high, with dry-stone walls up to fifteen feet thick, these massive Celtic structures included chambers, galleries, stairs—and often an excellent view, if only for security purposes.

Dun Aengus fort on Ireland's Inishmore Island sits on the edge of a sheer precipice overhanging the thundering breakers of the Atlantic Ocean pounding 250 feet below. Unlike traditional Celtic oppidas of earth and wood, the massive defense wall of this fort was built entirely of stone. Soil is so scarce on the island that farmers of recent times have removed it by hand from rocky crevasses and placed it on more open ground as patches for cultivation. In the way of many such ancient Celtic structures, no one today knows the name of this fort's king or chief, nor anything of the loves and often dramatic lives its inhabitants must have known.

9

The Taking of Britain

Third Roman Invasion Of Britain

In 43 A.D. the third and last invasion of Britain by Rome was ordered by the emperor Claudius. Now the Empire was at the height of its power, and this time the Romans would occupy Britain for four centuries. That's how long it would take the German tribes of northern Europe to do some invading of their own, eventually attacking Italy and Rome itself.

Unfortunately for the *divine*[1] Claudius, his thirteen-year reign was not long enough for him to witness the final conquest of Celtic Britain. It took over forty years and was not complete—the Romans never did conquer the people of Scotland in the north of the island.

In 83 A.D. the Roman general Agricola stared across the Irish Sea at the visible coast of Ireland with thoughts of adding to his glory. It was tempting, but he knew that if Scotland was difficult to conquer, Ireland would be even more so. By then the younger legionaries involved in the conquest of Britain had been born 20 years after it started.

With a force of 25,000 legionaries and the same number of auxiliaries—a total of 50,000 experienced troops—there was little doubt about the outcome of Rome's third invasion of Britain. As in Caesar's time a hundred years earlier, the island's Celtic inhabitants were divided into politically independent kingdoms. For this reason the Roman military

---

[1] Unlike Julius Caesar, the emperor Claudius was deified *during* his lifetime.

commander, Aulus Plautius, working as one with his single-minded, follow-the-leader soldiers, would find the Britons vulnerable to the strategy of "divide and conquer." Some Britons even sought the Romans' help to fight other Britons who were their enemies. Consequently, although they had to fight many battles, the Romans never did have to face a combined Briton army, thus making it possible to take most of the island section by section—which they ultimately did.

Romans invading Britain in 43 A.D. encountered these fourteen Celtic-speaking but politically separate Celtic kingdoms:

> Altrebates, Belgae (who gave their name to Belgium), Cantii (who gave their name to England's Kent), Catuvellauni, Coritani, Dobuni, Dumnonii (who gave their name to County Devon), Durotriges, Iceni, Noviomagi, Parisii (whose Gaulish branch gave their name to Paris, France), Regni, Silures, Trinovantes....

In earlier times the Greek, Strabo, writing of the continental Celts, counted no less then sixty Celtic groups in "Celtica," a Greek term for the great lands of the Celts that he knew of in his day. The number of kingdoms in Britain, however, was not the only confusing aspect of Celtic society encountered by the Romans in Britain.

Women Had Equal Rights; Elected As Rulers

The patriarchal Romans were surprised to find that the Celtic system of electing leaders in Britain did not exclude women from becoming society's highest ranking persons. Such were the Celtic queens of Britain, Cartimandua and Boudicca.

There were many violent confrontations between Romans and Britons during the forty-one years of conquest. Perhaps the most famous of these was when Britain's Celtic Queen Boudicca in A.D. 61 led the Iceni against the invaders in a sweeping revolt across southeast Britain, burning Roman London and destroying the Roman army's Ninth Legion along the way. It took ten years for Rome to regain the control it lost to this Celtic defender of early Britain. In recognition, the modern English in the twentieth century finally erected a great statue of Queen Boudicca riding her chariot. This monument stands in a place of honor, on the bank of the Thames next to London's Big Ben and the Houses of Parliament.

Yet another violent encounter in Britain, smaller but significant, was recorded by the Roman historian, Tacitus. He describes a scene of 59 A.D. in which a Roman army paused to look across the narrow Menai Strait at the Welsh island of Anglesey, where a group of Britons was preparing to defend themselves. Among those on the island, Tacitus wrote, a band of white-robed druids were "lifting up their hands to heaven and pouring forth horrible imprecations." He also said that women in black were dashing madly among the people like Furies, their hair in disarray and flaming torches in their hands. (It is not clear whether these women were supposed to be "druidesses.")

Tacitus the Roman smugly ends his story with the information that both druids and worshippers were killed "and their sacred groves dedicated to inhuman superstitions and barbarous rites destroyed."

Secondhand Story

Tacitus failed to mention that not only was he elsewhere during the Anglesey massacre, but that he was only four years old when it happened. The only people who knew exactly what they were doing on Anglesey were the Britons themselves. We have only a biased, one-sided version of their slaughter and the desecration of their sanctuary from an enemy who was not even there.

One modern textbook on the Celts, seemingly with as much bias as Tacitus, surprisingly refers to the activity of the druids on Anglesey as representing "fanatical antagonism to Rome." Another modern scholar writing on the Celts saw in the incident "that ritual cursing was another means of invoking divine wrath when needed." These statements, if applied with equal bias, would make fanatics and "ritual cursers" out of modern Christian pastors who threaten sinners and even their law-abiding flocks with God's wrath.

"History" Versus Fact

What Tacitus and others failed or did not want to recognize was that the slaughtered druids were not only learned holy men performing their priestly duties, but that they were ultimately non-combatant Briton patriots who gave their lives for their people and their country. The Romans naturally did not wish to see themselves as the marauding invaders they were. It was clear that the Pantheon, built by the Romans in 27 B.C. as a temple to honor all gods, was not meant to include the Celtic gods.

In destroying the Celtic religion, the Romans were being typically efficient in striving toward their imperial goals. They recognized, as Caesar had a century earlier in Gaul, that only the druids with their national and even international organization were capable of bringing the Celtic people together into a single and therefore dangerous force. Rome wanted Britain, and the druids had to go. To the Romans, the ultimate solution was to kill them—and they did.

Another theory says that the quest for booty lay behind the Roman attack on the druid center on Anglesey. Rome had invaded Britain because of its famed wealth in cattle, grain, hunting dogs and slaves. The item most central to Celtic wealth, however, was gold—as mined and exported by the Celts of Ireland. Archaeologists Ann Ross and Don Robins suggest that the Romans were aware that Anglesey Island was a key part of an important trade route from Ireland to mainland Europe via Britain. In such a scenario, the Roman military forces were after Irish gold stored by the druids on the island. This is probably correct, but it does not explain the merciless annihilation which Tacitus indicated was imposed on the druids of Anglesey.

Despite his prejudices, Tacitus produced important works and indeed has been judged by critics as Rome's most illustrious historian. Even Thomas Jefferson revered him as the "first writer in the world without a single exception."

Although, like other classical historians, Tacitus himself probably never saw a druid, he did at least know his fellow Romans and was forthright enough to criticize them when he thought they deserved it. On one occasion or another, among other things, he accused the Romans of "tyranny, injustice, debauchery, arson, desecration, adultery, torture, cruelty, corruption, and depravity."

Of the Roman army and its sacking of (Italian) Cremona, Tacitus wrote:

> "Aged men and women near the end of life, though despised as booty, were dragged off to be the soldiers' sport. Whenever a young woman or a handsome youth fell into their hands, they were torn to pieces by the violent struggles of those who tried to secure them, and this in the end drove the despoilers to kill one another."

Romans Kill Romans, Display Hacked-Off Heads

In describing the killing of Roman Emperor Galba and his supporters in 69 A.D., Tacitus wrote that their bodies lay in heaps, their heads displayed on poles. Galba's own head was cut off and his body "abused with a thousand insults." His head was maltreated and also displayed publicly on a pole. It disappeared for a night, for what reason nobody knows, but was found the next day and placed with what was left of the body. Rome had four different emperors in the year 69 A.D.

All of which is irrelevant to the Celts except that it shows an interesting aspect of the Romans who fought them for centuries and who wrote that the Celts were known to cut off the heads of their enemies.

CELTS UNDER THE ROMANS

Celts Appointed To Roman Senate

Roman rulers sometimes administered their newly conquered provinces in a relatively benign way that was in sharp contrast to the military ruthlessness applied in winning them. Less than a hundred years after Caesar had killed more than a million men, women and children in France, the survivors' descendants in that country had become so acculturated that some Celts became Roman senators. Records show that Domitius Afer, a Celt in the Roman province of Gaul, was made a *praetor* or judge in 25 A.D., and was later appointed consul—the same rank held by Caesar when he was placed in charge of all Gaul. In Austria, another Celt, Valerius Asiaticus, was appointed consul by Rome—twice. The Celts of continental Europe and Britain may have been subjugated, but they were certainly not annihilated. The considerable number of Celts remaining in northern Italy (in what had been Cisalpine Gaul) in time found their former territory called *Gallia Togata*—the land of the Celts who wear the toga. From these Romanized Celts came various "Latin" writers whose Celtic heritage was sometimes obscured. Scholars believe that Virgil (born in Cisalpine Gaul 70 B.C.) who wrote the Roman world's most famous epic, the *Aeneid*, was a Celtic writer.

With their acceptance of Roman rule, many Celtic chiefs in Britain were encouraged to remain in direct control of their individual tribes and territories, the boundaries of which were conveniently adopted by the Romans for administration purposes. The quick-learning Celts soon mastered the Roman language, written and oral. For the younger generation, schools were established (as they were in other formerly Celtic territories) which Roman children attended along with children of the Celtic aristocrats in fraternal togetherness. For centuries to come, these events contributed greatly to the spread of Latin as Europe's language of the literate.

Christianity Arrives

It is generally accepted that "organized" Christianity began in Rome with the arrival there of the apostle Paul in 61 A.D. Yet it was not until three centuries after the birth of Christ that the so-called "Edict of Milan" established Christianity as the religion of the Roman Empire—even if paganism in Rome continued with the vestal virgins still watching over their undying fire and others continuing to celebrate the feast of the *Great Mother*. Finally in 392 A.D. the emperor Theodosius established intolerance for religions other than Christianity by issuing an edict making "paganism" illegal. Christianity took root in Ireland and Britain from the third century A.D.

Benefits: Roman Citizenship And Villas

Some of the Celtic Briton aristocracy officially accepted Roman citizenship and learned to like living in Roman-style villas as their Celtic cousins did in Gaul. Ordinary Celtic Britons were welcomed as Roman citizens on completing service in the Roman army. Being left with the land they had always owned, the Celts of Britain were hardly a downtrodden people in the three and a half centuries of the *pax Romano* that followed the bloody invasion of their island.

Celts In Roman Army

In the years of Roman-occupied Britain, the Celtic chiefs and their followers freely adopted Roman names and fought alongside Roman armies. An integral part of the Roman strategy was to have the conquered Celtic overlords share in protecting the Roman province against others who might want to invade it. For the Romans it was impractical to hold this remote and vulnerable island at the edge of the world without a system of using the Celtic Britons themselves to defend it. Over the years such a defense was necessary against both the Picts from Scotland, and the various Teutonic or Germanic peoples who frequently attacked Britain from across the North Sea (which the Romans realistically if not ominously called *Oceanus Germanicus*—German Sea). It was yet other German tribes invading Italy to the south who would eventually force the Romans, after nearly four centuries, to abandon Britain once again to its Celtic inhabitants.

Who were these Germans who would destroy the mighty Roman Empire?

Celtic Origin Of The Words "German" And "Teuton"

First used in the fourth century B.C., the word *Teuton* or *Teutonic* is derived from the Celtic word meaning "people," as in the Irish *tuath*, and in the name of the Celtic (Gaulish) deity, *Teutaltes*. At one time used in referring to an otherwise nameless Germanic tribe in Jutland (Denmark), the words Teuton and Teutonic, thus borrowed from the Celts (and given the Latin form *Teutones* by the Romans), came to pertain to the wide-ranging northern Europeans which included the German, Dutch, Scandinavian, and related peoples. They are all Teutonic or *Germanic*.

Professors Powell and Cunliffe are among those who quote Dionysius Halicarnassus in his *Roman Antiquities* (written at the end of the first century B.C. but quoting older sources), describing that part of Celtica lying beyond the Rhine as *Germania*, apparently identifying it with Celts of that name who lived there. Such Celtic people appear to have been politically dominant over non-Celtic "German" tribal groups in their domain. These tribal groups did not know themselves as Germans (or Germani), nor did they appear to have any other collective name for themselves as a people. Indeed the people coming from that area in later centuries would call themselves by such names as Vandals, Goths, Franks, Saxons and others. Until about the time of Julius Caesar, *any* people invading from the Celtic lands to the east of the Rhine were *Germani*. Thus it is believed that the words German, Germany and Germanic are derived from the name of the Celts called the Germani who once lived east of the Rhine in what is now Germany. At about this time in early history, the Germans were semi-nomadic versus the settled Celtic farmers who built complex fortified settlements. Tacitus says that the Germans had little patience with organized agriculture and would move as the ground became exhausted. There was, however, much intermingling between the Germans and Celts. Ross and Robins write that there is evidence of a Celtic aristocracy influencing some Germanic areas. Some tribes considered to be German spoke Celtic and vice versa. Powell, in referring to the existence of Celtic loan words in German, gives as examples the words *reich* (as in state), and *amt* (as in state office), both derived from Celtic and significant in view of the Celts' political dominance. Physical descriptions of the Germanic and Celtic peoples were approximately the same, although not all classical historians were objective.

Writing as a prejudiced adversary more than historian, Tacitus, himself of Mediterranean ancestry, said that the Teuton (Germanic) warriors had "wild, blue eyes, reddish hair and huge frames that excel only in violent effort." He had good reason to be prejudiced, for it was the Germans who would finally beat the Romans at their own game and destroy the Roman Empire.

The Picts

Historically the Picts were a people occupying northeast Scotland during the Roman occupation of Britain. Despairing of ever subduing them, the Romans, in a vain attempt to stop their devastating raids into the south, built a wall (Hadrian's Wall) right across Britain to cut Scotland off from the rest of the island. They had a custom of painting their bodies, and their name means "painted people" in Latin, though they called themselves *Cruithne*.

A mysterious people about whom little is known, the Picts' language appears to have been a mixture of Celtic and some older speech. Their symbolic art is carved into stones found throughout northern Scotland. Many attempts to interpret the symbols have failed. Picts and the Celtic Scots united in about 842 A.D. and thereafter Pictish culture disappeared.

THE END OF ROMANO-CELTIC BRITAIN

The fragility of Rome's hold on Britain showed clearly in 367 A.D. when larger numbers than usual of Germanic raiders entered the island from the continent. They were beaten back only with difficulty by the combined Romano-Celtic forces. At the same time, Romanized Britain was being raided by Picts from Scotland and by seafaring Celts from Ireland. Along with rebelling Celts in Gaul, and German tribes thrusting against her northern borders, the Roman Empire no longer seemed invincible.

Britain progressively ceased to be a Roman province in the early fifth century A.D. as the West Roman Empire itself began to disintegrate. In 406 A.D. Germanic auxiliaries in the Roman army came to recognize their own great strength. They annihilated Roman frontier troops and swarmed far south into the Romano-Celtic provinces of France and Spain and threatened Rome—which in desperation withdrew her troops from Britain in 407 A.D.

Letter From The Mistress Of The World

Even with invaders on his own threshold, the emperor Honorius in 410 A.D. was honorable enough to send a now famous letter to the Romanized Celtic inhabitants of distant Britain in which he formally relinquished control of the island, telling them that they must henceforth look after their own defense. In the same year Rome, "the mistress of the world," was sacked by the Goths (800 years after the Celts sacked Rome in 390 B.C.). Finally, in 476 A.D. Rome's last emperor of the West, Romulus Augustulus, was deposed by the Goths.

The Celtic Britons were free of Rome, but not secure. The Irish Celts were forcefully establishing colonies in Wales and Cornwall, and the Picts, although probably half Celtic themselves, were continuing their attacks from Scotland. Most dangerous of all were the various Germanic tribes across the narrow *Oceanus Germanicus*—now the North Sea. For generations they had raided Britain's coast as hit-and-run marauders. Now with the Romans gone from the island, and with population figures and social tensions building among their own numbers, various Germanic tribes were to find Celtic Britain compellingly attractive.

The Celts Hire German Mercenaries

With threats of invasion from three directions, the Celts of Britain did what the Romans had done before them—they supplemented their own defense forces with mercenary troops from among the German Saxons. What occurred afterwards was described by Saint Gildas, a Welsh monk, in whose mind, as a literate Christian, the illiterate, non-Latin-speaking, non-Christian Germans were "barbarians" and "pagans."

> "The Saxon mercenaries," Gildas said, "soon complained that their monthly payments were not enough, threatening that if they were not given greater provisions and land they would attack the whole island...."

The Saxon mercenaries were given provisions, and land in Kent, but with their numbers greatly augmented by waves of other Saxon adventurers, they ignored their treaty and proceeded to plunder the land. After years of fighting and widespread devastation, the Britons eventually defeated the invaders in a decisive battle at Mount Badon in 500 A.D. But more and more Germans poured into the island. They had become a burgeoning nation in need of new land. In time the Romano-Celts were either overwhelmed or absorbed, or they retreated from western England to Wales or Cornwall and Brittany—thus forming, with Ireland, the "Celtic fringe" of Europe. Gildas, who died in 570, founded the monastery that bears his name in Brittany, France.

Although subdued for a time by Caesar's legions, France's Brittany had been a Celtic stronghold for centuries when the Germanic tribes invaded Britain. It was only natural that many Britons fleeing from the Saxon invaders should migrate there. Brittany is also known as *Breton*, its inhabitants being known as Bretons. The region changed its name from *Armorica* to "Brittany" (which means "little Britain") in about 500 A.D. with the arrival of large numbers of Briton Celts from Britain. Today's Brittany has retained numerous Celtic customs and traditions. Costumes featuring high lace headdresses are still worn on Sundays and holidays. French is the national language, but many Bretons are bilingual and also speak the Celtic language, known as Breton.

Bede The Venerable

An English, seventh-century Benedictine monk named Bede the Venerable—or Saint Bede—compiled, in Latin, virtually a summary of the learning of his day. Credited with having conducted careful research in the manner of modern scholars, he recorded valuable information on Britain's early and obscure years of the Middle (or "Dark") Ages following the fall of the Roman Empire and the invasions of Germanic tribes. He began the dating of historical events from the birth of Jesus rather than from the supposed creation of the world. He spent his life from the age of seven in the monastery at Jarrow. In 1899 he was canonized by Pope Leo XIII.

Origin Of The English People

In writing of the Teutonic tribes which invaded Britain after the Romans departed, Bede provided a historic description of the origin of the English people:

> "The newcomers," Bede wrote, "came from three very powerful German tribes, namely the Saxons, the Angles, and the Jutes.... In a short time, as bands from these tribes came to the island, they began to increase so much that they became a source of terror to the very natives who had invited them."

Members of these and other lesser known Germanic tribes (together with the Celts they assimilated), became the English people. Consequently the English are a Germanic people who speak a Germanic language called English.

Origin Of The Words "England" And "English"

England and the English take their name directly from the *Angle* tribe (hence Angle-land, which eventually became Eng-land or England). They were a Germanic people who, as described by Bede, invaded Britain in the fifth century A.D. at about the same time as the German Saxons.

Although not the most numerous of the Teutonic peoples who then settled in Britain, the Angles' particular invasion was led by members of the Anglian royal house. Their name and its desired "royal" connotation was favored and adopted by all the Germanic inhabitants of the island by the sixth century.

The Angles, while they were still all on mainland Europe, were one of the barbarous German tribes mentioned by the Roman historian, Tacitus. He described their rituals in which they sacrificed people to the Mother Earth goddess. Some extraordinarily well preserved bodies of such victims of violence have recently been discovered in Danish peat bogs. Popularly known as the *bog people*, or swamp corpses (*Moorleichen*), they are apparently of the same tribe that gave its name to the English.

The sixteenth-century hyphenation of "Angle" and "Saxon" into the term *Anglo-Saxon* is now loosely used to denote any Caucasian people (or their descendants) of the "British" Isles. Descendants of the Saxons and the Angles who did not cross the North Sea into Britain in the fifth and sixth centuries still live in Germany's Saxony and Schleswig-Holstein regions.

King Arthur: Defender Of Britain Against The English

One of the few things known about the legendary King Arthur, based on scraps of historical evidence, is that he was a Celtic leader of Britain when it was still a Celtic land. A staunch Christian, he was said to have fought twelve battles throughout Britain around 500 A.D., becoming a Briton hero for his stand against the pagan Saxons and other Germanic peoples invading the island. Arthur eventually died in battle against them. Yet the resistance of other Celts following his example denied much of Celtic Britain to the invaders for fifty years, and most of Wales and Cornwall for centuries.

The legend of Arthur, originating in the kind of imaginative Celtic energy that created the Irish "heroic" sagas, established him as the supremely valorous Christian knight and (Celtic) king of Britain who led his mounted warriors against the enemies of his country. Over the years the legend grew in complexity while becoming one of Europe's most loved and famous stories. English, French and German writers added to the original story. Yet in every respect and in all versions Arthur continues to resemble the classical Celtic warrior-hero who had been created and idealized throughout Europe in Celtic society for centuries in the past, and perpetuated by them, and by others in imitation, for centuries to come.

What Winston Churchill Said Of The King Arthur Legend

> "We...find ourselves in the presence of a theme as well founded, as inspired, and as inalienable from the inheritance of mankind as the *Odyssey* or the Old Testament. It is all true, or ought to be; and more and better besides. And wherever men are fighting against barbarism, tyranny, and massacre, for freedom, law, and honor, let them remember that the fame of their deeds, even though they themselves be exterminated, may perhaps be celebrated as long as the world rolls round. Let us declare that King Arthur and his noble knights, guarding the Sacred Flame of Christianity and the theme of a world order...slaughtered innumerable hosts of foul barbarians and set decent folk an example for all time."
>
> (*A History of the English-Speaking Peoples*, vol. 1)

Ironically, the "foul barbarians" referred to by Churchill were the Anglo-Saxons in the process of becoming the English.

Famous Arthurian Characters

In various versions of King Arthur's story, elaborated by British, French and German writers, he was born the illegitimate son of a Briton (Celtic) king of Britain and raised in secrecy. Withdrawing a sword embedded in a stone proved his right to the throne, and he reigned in his court at Camelot with his Queen Guinevere, attended by his court magician, Merlin, a "modern" druid for his time. The possessor of the miraculous sword, *Excalibur*, given him by the mysterious Lady of the Lake, Arthur became known as a noble king and great warrior.

Among his enemies were his nephew, Mordred, and his sister, Morgan le Fay, an evil sorceress who plotted to win Arthur's throne for herself and her lover. Two of the more noble characters who sat at Arthur's famous Round Table were the knights, Sir Lancelot of the lake and Sir Tristan. Both became involved in tragic love affairs, Lancelot with Arthur's Queen Guinevere, and Tristan with Isolde, the Irish queen of Tristan's Welsh uncle, King Mark of Cornwall.

In the Arthurian medieval world, chivalric code and courtly romance demanded that young gentlemen were to fall in love with unattainable virgins or married ladies. Only after suffering months of silence could they proclaim their love, then prove it by performing noble deeds and quests. Lancelot's son, Sir Galahad (Parsifal in some versions), became the hero of the quest for the *Holy Grail*.

The Holy Grail

The object known as the *Holy Grail* was a chalice or bowl associated with medieval legend and literature and popularly identified with the chalice used by Jesus at the Last Supper. Supposed to have been brought to England by Saint Joseph of Arimathea, it was said to be miraculous in its powers and could provide food and healing.

This concept of a miraculous chalice or bowl may well have been derived from the magical *Cauldron of the Dagda* of ancient Celtic mythology. The Dagda (the Good One), a deity considered to be "father" to the Celtic people, was always associated (as seen in surviving ancient sculptures) with a great cauldron which had properties of unlimited sustenance, rejuvenation, and inspiration. The Cauldron of the Dagda probably came to be the Holy Grail after Christianity reduced Dagda to a mere pagan god. This deity was known as Dagda in Ireland, and as *Sucellos* in Celtic Gaul.

A Celtic Legacy

Early writers in Britain, including twelfth-century authors Wace, Layamon, and Geoffrey of Monmouth, lovingly embellished the Arthur legend, as did medieval German poets Wolfram von Eschenbach and Gottfried von Strasburg, among others. Twelfth-century French authors Marie de France and Chretien de Troyes acknowledged Celtic sources for their writing inspiration, with both of them writing their own versions of the King Arthur story. Many great medieval literary works are poetic elaborations of old Celtic legends.

In thirteenth-century Germany, Gottfried von Strasburg, selecting his own favorite characters from the King Arthur legend, chose to write a poem about the love union between Queen Isolde and Tristan—the Celtic knight who, although noble in spirit, was all too human after all. Much later, in nineteenth-century Germany, composer Richard Wagner used this immortal story of a tragic Celtic love affair for his famous opera, *Tristan und Isolde*.

In America, Mark Twain would write "A Connecticut Yankee in King Arthur's Court," a novel about a New England mechanic going back to sixth-century England. The modern American author Persia Woolley has written a trilogy of Arthurian books in which the magic of Camelot is presented through the eyes of the free-spirited Celtic girl who becomes the strong-minded and earthy High Queen Guinevere, "the heroine of hundreds of legends" in her own right. The second book includes "a London bustling in preparation for the Round Table Council" and "the mystical revelry of ancient Druid ceremonies."

King Arthur Arrives In Las Vegas

A perpetuation of the King Arthur legend was grandly represented by the 1990 opening of the Excalibur Hotel and Casino in Las Vegas. Guests, who are promised to have their "days enhanced by knights," are entertained by dinner shows featuring King Arthur with knights and horses in jousting and sword fighting action in a 1,000-seat amphitheater. This awe-inspiring, castellated Camelot soaring spectacularly out of the Nevada desert includes a "royal" village with seven theme restaurants and a "Renaissance Faire" area. The Excalibur has 4,032 guest rooms, making it one of the world's largest hotels.

Durability Of Arthur, Celtic King Of Britain

Arthur and his noble knights formed a large part of medieval romance. The stories, reaching places as far away as Iceland and Italy, and even the Middle East, helped to illuminate European society's way through the Dark Ages. If they were not true, as the Anglo-American Winston Churchill said, they "ought to be."

With all the versions of his story, which included such distractions as enchanted castles, distressed damsels, magic springs, evil giants and crafty dwarfs, King Arthur has always remained at the center of the Celtic legend that bears his name. Through this Celtic heritage, left to Britain and the world, a central part of the teachings and values of the ancient Celts survived in the medieval Christian chivalric code of fair play, and from there, in one form or another, indefinitely into the future.

10

CELTIC BARDS, SAINTS AND SCHOLARS

Britain And Ireland After The Romans

In the years following the Anglo-Saxon invasion of Britain, the Celtic Britons who remained in Cornwall, Wales and Scotland included the only Christians and Latin-educated people left on the island.

For generations the pagan Anglo-Saxon invaders divided their half of Britain into the often feuding and separate English kingdoms of Kent, East Anglia, Mercia, Northumbria, Essex, Sussex, and Wessex. At about the same time the Celtic people of Ireland were also divided into various kingdoms.

The Romans never invaded neighboring Ireland during the four centuries they ruled Britain. When they finally left Britain in the fifth century A.D., Ireland was still inhabited by a Celtic people who had never been subjugated by any other nation. Their language and oral literature came directly from the ancient Celts of mainland Europe.

The Irish Celts had continued to be a traditionally "heroic" society, complete with impressive war chariots, fearless aristocratic knights and, ideally, one-to-one combat where the best man won. Such representative or symbolic confrontations were often preferred by the early Celts over the wasteful slaughter of outright battles.

A preoccupation with the past and present exploits of warriors gave the period its name, *Age of Heroes*. Folklore told of mothers giving their male children their first food on the tips of their fathers' swords, vowing that they should find no death but in battle.

When not raiding each other for cattle or land, there were such diversions for the warriors as bird hunting or perhaps even riding to hounds with the king. It was a Celtic way of life that had never known the imperial ambitions of the Romans or the territorial demands of the Teutones.

With their numerous independent kingdoms, the people of Ireland in the early centuries A.D. never did have a national military or political force under a single "high" king or sovereign. As with the early Anglo-Saxons in Britain, a man's allegiance was owed to his own local king and no one else. Yet ancient manuscripts from the seventh and eighth centuries (which recorded oral histories of previous centuries) show that all who lived on the island had long considered themselves "people of Ireland." Besides speaking a common language, they shared a common history based on ancient legend, and also shared a finely detailed common code of law (*Brehon Law*).

Brehon Law: How It Worked

Brehon Law was based on the principle that men should be responsible to one another rather than to the impersonal institution of the state. Under this system, wrongdoing was not a civil offense but a violation of private rights. A person who harmed or injured another was made to pay his debt to the injured person or to his family, and not to society as a whole. This system of law and the institutions of the learned classes prevailed in Irish society from prehistoric times until the Tudor conquest a thousand years later. A part of this law system dealt with the running of hospitals at which no person, sick, old, poor, or orphaned, could be turned away without treatment. Irish physicians and medical schools were renowned in Europe. Peter Ellis writes that surviving Irish medical documents are regarded as the largest collection of medical literature before the nineteenth century existing in any language.

"Brehon Law" is a name derived from the title borne by its practitioners, *brithem*, the Irish word for "judge" (who in former times may have been druid judges). This customary law of the Celtic peoples was highly developed and, in earlier centuries, passed on orally with great accuracy from generation to generation by professional jurists. These jurists were a part of the highly regarded professional class of learning and art in Irish society whose members could pass freely among all the people. After the introduction of Christianity they included historians, musicians, poets and bards.

POETS WITH POWER

To describe the bards of early Ireland would probably be close to describing the Celtic bards of ancient Bavaria, Switzerland, France, and of Britain. Diodorus Siculus wrote that "the bards of Gaul sang to instruments like lyres, sometimes a eulogy, sometimes a satire." The sophistication of Celtic eloquence and rhetoric impressed Marcus Porcius Cato in the second century B.C.

The bards' power of satire was dreaded and their praise greatly desired. The reputation of a nobleman could be made or destroyed on their well-phrased words. To the Celts, who were extraordinary in having a god of eloquence—*Ogmios* (*Ogma* in pre-Christian Ireland), eloquence was considered more powerful than physical strength.

In such places as ancient Ireland and Wales, bards were members of an order who composed and sang the poems that celebrated the feats and genealogy of Celtic kings, chieftains and warriors. Regardless of their birth, these lyre-playing bards shared many privileges enjoyed by the nobility because they were an important professional class within their society. What they recorded orally (and passed on from generation to generation) was what formed the foundation for much Celtic thought and action. The highest-ranking kind of bard was known as an *Ollam* or teacher who moved about the country in the style of the nobility with a retinue of more than twenty followers.

Most bards seem to have been men, but at least one Irish story provides an exception (*Cathluina*). This story says that "The daughter of Moran seized the harp, and her voice of music praised the strangers. Their souls melted at the song, like the wreath of snow before the eye of the sun."

In Ireland the bards could recite poems thousands of lines long. They were responsible for perpetuating a vast oral anthology which not only included mythology, history, current events and vital genealogical records, but which were cleverly composed to entertain as well. In Germany, France, Britain and Ireland, the Celtic bards were the first historians these countries ever knew.

Ogham Writing

The earliest non-Latin documents of Britain and Ireland were written in the Celtic *Ogham* script. This form of writing was developed in Ireland just before the arrival there of Christianity, in about the fourth century. Although the *Book of Ballymote* had an Ogham tract, surviving examples of Ogham are usually inscriptions on memorial stones; 300 of them in Ireland, and 57 in Britain (the result of Irish migrations there). The stones are generally inscribed with the name of the person commemorated, often with details of his descent, if only his father's name. Ireland's Brehon Law recognized the use of Ogham as evidence of land ownership, thus giving it legal recognition and status.

The word "Ogham" is derived from *Ogma*, the Celtic god of eloquence. Ogham's twenty letters are short and long strokes touching or crossing a median line on which the inscription was cut—an ideal style for inscribing wood or stone for which it was probably designed. While it has been suggested that Ogham represents Latin letters, it is improbable that it was regularly used for any sustained literary effort. In a kind of poetry all its own, Ogham named each of its letters after a tree, with D, for instance, being represented by *daur*, an oak.

Ogham writings represent the earliest messages left to the modern people of Britain and Ireland directly from their ancestors before the adoption of Latin from the Romans. A few later examples are bilingual, being written in both Ogham and Latin. Some more recent stones are inscribed with a cross, denoting the use of Ogham into Christian times. But while Ogham writing documented in stone the names of a few hundred people, it was the learned classes in Ireland (at first the druids and the bards and later the semi-religious *filidh*) who were responsible for preserving countless generations of their people's history.

Bards were trained in organized schools where among other things they were required to memorize "chief" or king stories, and 100 sub-stories. Once graduated, however, each minstrel sang stories in his or her own way, adding to or shaping them in their own particular style.

Traditional bardic schools survived in Ireland into the tenth century. The time required to graduate was the same as Caesar reported for the former druids in Gaul—twenty years. Some "modern" bardic schools in Ireland existed into the seventeenth century.

Carolan, the old blind harper, called the last of the bards, died in 1738. Yet there was one even later. Ireland's *Mirror*, 1804, described Hennessey, a living seer, as the *Orpheus* of his country. (It is doubtful, however, if Hennessey could have equaled the mythological Orpheus' final feat when his severed head, still singing, floated across the Aegean sea to the island of Lesbos where, possibly, the rest of him was not greatly missed.)

Today's National *Eisteddfod* of Wales, an annual August festival with competitions among poets and musicians (a historical institution since the *twelfth* century), is a celebration of Celtic bardic traditions that is appreciated and supported by a modern British society.

As a people the Celts have always had a natural feeling for learning, intellectual concepts, and the eloquence of the spoken word. Classical writers praised the ancient Celts' elegant use of language and appreciation of linguistic subtlety. Among the Celts themselves, their learned intellectuals—the druids and the bards—were revered and welcomed everywhere and were free to pass unhindered from territory to territory. Today in Celtic society the scholar and the poet are still greatly respected (writers and other creative artists in modern Ireland are not required to pay income tax).

The Celtic tongue is one of the world's most complex languages; a result of its development for centuries around the requirements of a professional learned class, the druids and the bards. While other societies centered their activities and thoughts around the mundane essentials of daily survival, the Celts were developing speech and thought to a degree of eloquence that gained a reputation beyond their own borders.

Today scholars divide the Celtic language into two major branches, "P" Celtic as spoken in France and Wales, and "Q" Celtic or Gaelic as spoken in Ireland and Scotland (which was named after the Irish *Scotti* who settled it). Gaelic appears to be the oldest and most complex branch of the language, reflecting its wide-ranging history and the philosophical and scientific pursuits with which it was associated for centuries. The people of Ireland naturally call their Celtic language "Irish."

The Celts' affinity for learning continues into the present time, as indicated, for example, by Ireland's secondary school graduates being today better educated than their contemporaries in Britain. Some 30% of Ireland's school-leavers go on to further education, compared with 25% of Britons. Dublin's Trinity College was the first university in Europe to grant degrees to women. In recent years there has been a significant increase in the number of engineering degrees earned in the Republic of Ireland, with a 62% increase in computer science degrees.

In modern times visitors to Celtic countries have told stories of meeting farmers or other "ordinary" Irish, Scots, Welsh or Breton people who were capable of discoursing on philosophy or literature on a level more usually found among university graduates. Samuel Johnson, chief dictator of the literary tastes of his age, toured the Scottish Highlands in 1773 and later referred repeatedly to this phenomenon. It is probably no coincidence that when Britain's Philological Society contracted in 1879 with Oxford University's Oxford Press to produce the first edition of the *Oxford English Dictionary*, the university choose a Celt, a Scottish grammar school teacher named James A. H. Murray, to edit it. The latest edition of this ultimate dictionary runs into twenty volumes and sells for $2,500.

The Irish are known to have one of the highest standards of education in the world. This complements the presence in Ireland of many national and international industries and businesses, including German, Japanese, and American. Referring to Ireland's economy being the fastest growing in

Europe, and comparing it to some of the Pacific Rim countries in Asia, *The Wall Street Journal* and London's *Financial Times* have dubbed Ireland "the Celtic Dragon."

CELTIC VOYAGERS

A People At The End Of The Earth Who Liked To Travel

The Romans never reached Ireland; a place they considered to be at the precipitous edge of the world. To the Celts who settled Ireland, however, their island was perceived as just one of many lands suitable for habitation. Their original migration to the island had involved not only a seafaring technology, but an adventurous awareness that there were other worlds beyond their own to explore. As a people they had wandered a long way by land and sea from the Celtic heartland in continental Europe. It seems that curiosity and a love of travel were in the Celtic blood.

The Irish Invade Britain

From the third century A.D. Irish seafaring chieftains and their warriors were defying the Romans to raid western Britain. The sixteen-year-old Romanized Celt from Britain who would become Saint Patrick was just one of the many slaves Irish seafaring raiders took from Britain to work on Irish farms. But the Irish also sailed to Britain to form permanent settlements such as Dyfed in Wales which began a royal dynasty that lasted for five centuries. Dyfed is today still proudly named after this Irish kingdom. Another Irish kingdom was set up in Wales at Brecknock.

Origin Of The Name Scotland

From about the fourth century A.D., Irish Celts, known to the Romans as *Scotti*, invaded Britain's far north where they established permanent settlements. Eventually founding a kingdom there in the fifth century called *Dalriada*, the Irish Scotti ultimately gave their name to that part of Britain now known as Scotland. Today many people in Scotland continue to speak *Gaelic*, the Irish branch of the Celtic language—and to live in a country named after the Irish people who settled it. The earliest Latin name for Ireland was *Scotia*, which was eventually replaced with the latin name, *Hibernia*. For centuries the word *Scottus* as part of a person's name denoted being Irish or of Irish ancestry (see *Charlemagne And His Irish Scholars*, page 170).

The Voyage Of Saint Brendan

A seventh-century A.D. Latin text from an Irish monastery describes the sixth-century journey of a Celtic monk-explorer, Saint Brendan, who sailed from Ireland into the unknown reaches of the Atlantic in search of the Land of Promise of the Saints. The saga, known as *Navigatio Sancti Brendani Abbatis*—Voyage of Saint Brendan the Abbot—describes Saint Brendan with a crew of fellow monks reaching and returning from a distant land which some now believe to have been America. The description of the seven-year-long voyage included references to what may have been whales, volcanic eruptions (as occur in Iceland), and icebergs, which are commonly found floating southward with the Labrador Current along the coast of North America. Although the distant land discovered by Brendan the Navigator has never been verified as America, there is evidence in New England that Celtic visitors constructed megaliths there well before Columbus crossed the Atlantic in 1492. The *Navigatio* was eventually translated in continental European monasteries by Irish monks from Latin into other languages. Later explorers, including Columbus, were influenced by it.

Saint Brendan, who founded Clonfert Monastery in Ireland's County Galway, explored the Atlantic four centuries before the Vikings may have reached North America, and about nine centuries before Columbus. Galway is situated on Ireland's rugged west coast—the perfect departure point for Atlantic explorers. We know that the Celts were great boat builders, based on the discovery of the sixty-foot, masted Celtic vessel lying at the bottom of Lake Neuchâtel (see Chapter 2). Caesar wrote admiringly of the Celtic Breton (*Veneti*) seafarers whose coast, he said, "lies exposed to the violence of the open sea." He used Celtic-built ships to transport a Roman army of 10,000 men in his 55 B.C. invasion of Britain. It is not known if he sought the protection of *Manannan*, Celtic god of the sea.

Strabo mentioned the "force of the Atlantic winds" in describing the seaworthy, oak-built design of Celtic ships. No one knows precisely from where in Europe the Celts came to Ireland. One possibility is that they sailed from Brittany in their timber sailing vessels which have been described as up to 150 feet long with a beam of sixteen feet. The *Mayflower* which carried the Pilgrims from England to America in 1620 was only about ninety feet long.

Saint Brendan's Voyage Re-Enacted

Using Irish technology and materials of the sixth century, a thirty-six-foot replica of Saint Brendan's skin-covered boat was constructed in modern times and successfully sailed from Ireland to North America by Timothy Severin and his crew. A Celtic Veneti craft of the type described by Strabo might have been a better idea for such an experiment. It also could possibly have been closer to what Saint Brendan would have used. The skin-covered coracles and *curraghs* traditionally used by the Irish until recent times may have been developed just for their island's inland waterways and the relatively calm coastal waters, long after their seafaring ancestors with much larger boats had settled in Ireland to become pastoralists and cultivators.

THE BEGINNING OF RECORDED HISTORY IN IRELAND

When the Pope crowned a German, Otto I, emperor of Rome in 962 A.D., the act formally created the *Holy Roman Empire*, a political entity that was a union of Germany and northern Italy. This Pope-solemnized coronation, following the crowning of Charlemagne as emperor of the West by Pope Leo III in 800 A.D., was an indication that Rome had long since risen from her political ashes to become the center of the Christian world. A German was emperor of the eternal city, but all of Christian Europe then looked to the Pope of Rome as its religious leader. In fact the Pope and the Christian faith had been internationally influential over much of Europe for centuries before the coronation of Otto I.

It could be said that the recorded history of Ireland began in 431 A.D. In that year Pope Celestine appointed a bishop named Palladius to the care of the Irish "believing in Christ." While there are few details of Palladius' mission, there must have been reason for Christian Rome to believe that Christianity had already started to replace paganism in Ireland.

It arrived gently, but when it came, Christianity would change the Irish way of life more than any invading army.

Saint Patrick: The Man Who Loved Ireland

There are no precise details about the origins of the man who, beginning life with the name of *Sucat*, became known to history as *Saint Patrick*. He was a Celt born somewhere on the west coast of Roman-occupied Britain in about 385 A.D., a time in history occurring before the invasion of that Celtic island by the Germanic Anglo-Saxon tribes, who would eventually become the English.

Captured and enslaved by Irish seafaring raiders when only sixteen, Patrick worked for six years as a herdsman in northern Ireland. Responding to a voice, he escaped and sailed to the once Celtic land of Gaul (France) where he studied at the monasteries of *Lerins* and *Marmoutiers*. There he was trained and eventually admitted into holy orders. A vision instructed him to return to Ireland and make it Christian. After spending a further twelve years at Auxerre studying to be a missionary, he went to Rome where he was appointed the second bishop with an apostolic mission for Ireland. Only then did he call himself *Patricius* or Patrick. In 432 A.D. he traveled to Ireland where he worked to convert the island to Christianity. Ireland, which had become partly Christianized before the arrival of Patrick, was a country where Christianity took root without the shedding of blood.

Working with a band of followers, Patrick was extraordinarily successful, converting kings and commoners alike. The story of his driving the snakes out of the island is symbolic, relating to his effectiveness in driving out paganism.

Shrine Of Saint Patrick Destroyed By The English

Shortly before his death in Ireland in about 461 A.D. Patrick climbed to the peak of one of Ireland's highest mountains from where he blessed all the people of the country. Today he is Ireland's patron saint, and the mountain he climbed (*Croaghpatrick*) is named after him.

Saint Patrick was buried in Downpatrick, which was a great European shrine until its destruction by the English government in 1539.

Paganism Exchanged For Christianity

While early Christian missionaries from Rome encountered only rudimentary elements of law and learning among the Germanic peoples in the fifth century A.D., they found that Irish society included organized schools which had for centuries produced learned and respected specialists in religion, calendrical skills, law, genealogy, poetry and oral literature. When Ireland replaced paganism with Christianity, the Celtic high regard for knowledge and learning not only remained, but flourished more than ever with the added dimension of writing.

With the adoption of Christianity, ancient Celtic Ireland emerged from its *Age of Heroes* and entered its *Age of Saints*, becoming known to the rest of Europe as the *Island of Saints*. (At that time a holy man could be given the title of "Saint" without in fact being a saint canonized by Rome.)

From the sixth century the Irish became internationally known for their devotion to learning and scholarly activities and for actively spreading their knowledge and civilization abroad. The Celts, despite an alleged fondness for war, had been fascinated with organized learning and knowledge for centuries. That was what their druids and bards were all about. The early Christian monasteries in Ireland were the natural successors to the druid and bardic schools.

Europe's Oldest Vernacular Literature After Greek And Latin

In pre-Christian times, the bards and druids collectively kept intact the traditional knowledge of their people, faithfully passing it down through the generations. By the sixth century A.D. there were Irish monks who were educated in both the Latin of their profession and in the traditional learning of their people. Using the Roman alphabet, they created a written form of the ancient Irish language in which they recorded their peoples' laws, legends and poetry before they were lost forever. What they wrote down is historically Europe's oldest vernacular literature after Greek and Latin.

It took hundreds of years for the bards and historians of pre-Christian Ireland to acquire their collective knowledge. Today the only surviving knowledge from them is what was eventually recorded of their oral literature by these early Irish monks who may well have known the more popular stories by heart. It is thought that some monks themselves may have been former bards.

During the Roman occupation of Britain, Irish society was dominated by a warrior class aristocracy whose exploits would provide much of the material in countless ballads, poems, and lengthy sagas. Many of these were transcribed in later centuries to become one of the greatest heroic traditions of European literature. The Celts made their heroes into gods and their gods into heroes. A fighting spirit was much valued and admired—even in death. One story told of a king asking to be buried upright with his sword in hand facing the enemy. His people became unbeatable until the enemy re-buried him in a prone position.

Magic, Love And Nature

Not all Irish stories, however, were about heroic warriors. There were haunting tales of love and nature, and of magic, humor, satire, religion, and even current affairs. Some poems were touching elegies. Many Irish bardic songs survived to become part of the repertoire of medieval troubadours in other countries. In Ireland they may have helped to inspire Yeats and Joyce in their time.

Celtic Goddesses Who Made Kings, Not Babies

To the Celts, intellectual ability and supernatural prowess in their gods was more important than good looks. In the Irish sagas, young men frequently became kings by sleeping with ugly women who were really goddesses. The Irish hero, *Lugaid*, became a king by sleeping with a hag. The formidable *Queen Medb* of Connaught, who was said to be both divine and loathsome, claimed to have been thus instrumental in the placing of nine Irish kings.

Ireland's Most Famous Story

The epic story, *Táin Bó Cualnge* (The Cattle Raid of Cooley) is the best known of all Irish tales and one of the greatest prose sagas of the ancient world. Celtic society's respect for rules and integrity is demonstrated through its hero, *Cú Chulainn*.

Ireland's First Censors

It was not by chance that Irish monks transcribed the oral literature of their people. Even after the introduction of Christianity, the Irish sagas were still accorded great prestige and importance. Yet some scribes could not resist writing "modern" comments on the compositions of their pagan ancestors, sometimes entering them on the margins of their transcriptions.

A pious Christian monk, who had just fondly written down the *Táin Bó Cualnge*, wrote a personal note saying that he did not believe everything he read in it. "Some things," he said, "are the work of the devil, some are poetic inventions, some are true, and some are meant for the delight of fools."

Responsible for preserving much of the ancient oral literature of Ireland, the church was also its first censor. It will never be known what extraordinary and unique parts were excised by individual scribes because they were considered incompatible with the new Christian thinking.

The Opinion Of A Modern Scholar

The distinguished Celtic authority, Professor Kenneth Jackson, who taught at the universities of Edinburgh, Cambridge, and Harvard, said of the creators of early medieval Celtic literature:

> "The most striking quality...is their power of vivid imagination and freshness of approach; as if every poet, gifted with a high degree of imaginative insight, rediscovered the world for himself. Where other medieval literatures are conventional and even hackneyed, early Celtic literature is capable of being highly original."

Early Irish Monasteries: Havens For Celtic Art

The Celtic love of learning and of creative skills readily found a home in Ireland's monasteries when Christianity became established on the island. The ancient arts gained new life as the creation of beautiful objects to glorify God became an extension of worship. Exquisite works of metal and stone were created by skilled and willing hands. Countless written compositions were produced in the monasteries' *scriptoria* or writing rooms. The subjects included astronomy, natural history, and religion. In a time long before the advent of printing, great importance was given to transcribing copies of the Gospels for use by the monasteries.

The Book Of Kells

Now an Irish national treasure and one of the most valuable books in the world, the *Book of Kells* was written by hand in Latin by Irish monks in the ninth century or earlier. The book may have been started in the Irish monastery at Iona, Scotland, before it was taken to Kells in Ireland for completion and protection from the Vikings. Although mainly containing the Gospels of Matthew, Mark, Luke and John, it also includes notes on local history. No less than 678 of the book's pages are brilliantly illuminated by hand in breathtaking, exquisitely detailed beauty; with elaborate, full-page color illustrations placed at the beginning of each Gospel and chapter.

Queen Victoria And The Book Of Kells

Clearly descended from the Hallstatt and La Tene cultures at their best, the artistry of the Book of Kells demonstrates a continuity in Celtic aesthetics going back at least to Switzerland in 500 B.C. Although sixty pages are missing, it is regarded as the finest surviving example of Celtic illuminated manuscript. It is on permanent display to the public at Trinity College, Dublin, where a new page is turned each day. Queen Victoria, on being shown the book while on a visit to Dublin, imperiously asked for a pen, expecting that she should sign it.

The *Book of Kells* was written and drawn by Irish monks in the 8th-9th centuries. Containing the Gospels of Matthew, Mark, Luke and John, its scintillating, exquisitely detailed, curvilinear style reflects a continuity of Celtic art going back to 750 B.C. in continental Europe. On this page, two Greek letters followed by a Latin letter represent the Latin word *Christi*. The small printed letters at the bottom right translate as "Now the birth of (Jesus) Christ..." A magnifying glass can reveal human and animal forms occasionally worked into the design. Courtesy: The Board of Trinity College, Dublin.

The Ardagh Chalice: Priceless Art Lost And Found

Any list of renowned Celtic metalwork must include the piece known as the Ardagh Chalice. Inscribed elegantly with the names of the apostles, this eighth-century A.D. marvel of Celtic artistry is considered to be among Ireland's most valuable art objects. A remarkable combination of techniques was required to make it, using gold, silver, and bronze, with rock crystal and glass set into the finest of La Tene decorations. It was found buried in a ring-fort by a boy digging for potatoes where it was probably hidden more than a thousand years earlier by monks to save it from plundering Vikings.

The Tara Brooch

Called after the site formerly occupied by Ireland's high kings, the *Tara Brooch* was in fact found many miles away on the seashore. Its materials are gold, silver, copper and glass. The processes of enameling, filigree, wire beading, granulation, inlaying and soldering were all used to make it. Tiny human faces illuminated in purple glass are surrounded by endless patterns. Made without the benefit of magnifying glasses or spectacles, it is a wonder of exquisitely fine metalwork produced at an Irish monastery. The monks who created it (and some other art of the period) may have used drops of water as magnifying "glasses."

The Tara Brooch incorporates much of what went into Celtic art down through the centuries—from at least 700 B.C. Made in about 700 A.D., it is today the most copied of all Celtic jewelry.

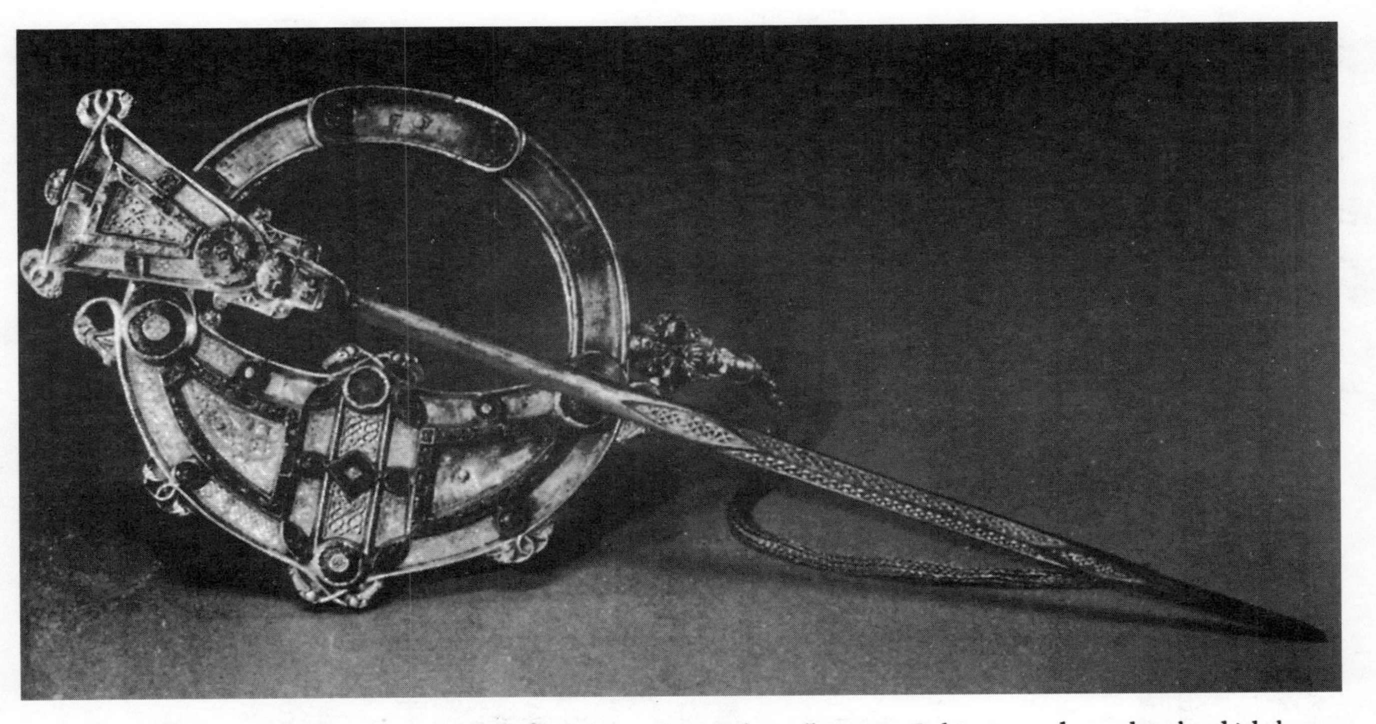

Ireland's eighth-century Tara Brooch continued the tradition of excellence in Celtic art and metalwork which began more than a thousand years earlier in continental Europe. Photo courtesy Bord Fáilte, Dublin, Ireland.

The Snettisham Torque

The Celtic-made necklet of this name is considered to be Britain's most beautiful antiquity. Made with precise detail, its main part consists of eighty-four gold wires twisted into eight strands. It serves as an exquisite symbol of Britain's Celtic heritage. Queen Boudicca was known to wear such an ornament while riding her chariot in war against Rome.

GOLDEN AGE OF SAINTS AND SCHOLARS

From the sixth to the ninth centuries A.D., Irish native excellence, representing the "purest" Celtic culture remaining in Europe, burst forth unrestrained in the literary and creative arts to secure a very special place in the history of European civilization. This included Ireland's *Golden Age of Saints and Scholars*, an extraordinary period which spread learning and Christianity throughout much of Europe like a guiding light in the Dark Ages after the fall of Rome. During these centuries, Ireland's monasteries are considered to have been the most brilliant centers of learning in all Europe.

Ireland's First Missionary To Britain

A hundred years after Saint Patrick's arrival in fifth-century Ireland, Irish Christian missionary monks were already spreading Christianity among the pagans of Anglo-Saxon England and the Romano-Celtic Britons of Wales and Scotland. The most famous of such monks was Saint Colum Cille, better known as Saint Columba. Like Saint Patrick, he is an authentic historic figure. Described as passionately devoted to learning and a master scribe, he founded an abbey on the Scottish island of Iona about 563 A.D. which would become famous in his lifetime and far beyond.

Born a prince of the Ui Neill and eligible for the kingship of Tara, Columba was partly educated in a bardic school. He played the harp, and poets were always affectionately welcomed by him. Even while known as a great abbot in Scotland, he was also respectfully called the "Chief Poet" of Ireland.

Loch Ness Monster, Saint Columba And The Druids

Famous personalities tend to attract all kinds of tales about them, some true, others fascinating but unprovable. One popular story describes Saint Columba dramatically holding at bay, with his upheld cross, a giant water creature which seems to have been the Loch Ness monster. Quite separately from this extraordinary event, Saint Columba was interestingly known to have referred to God as "My Druid," and to have said that "My Druid is Christ the Son of God."

On his death bed in 597 A.D., Saint Columba composed his own eulogy which historically became the earliest known Irish verse of undisputed authorship.

The Irish Spread Learning In Britain

From Iona and from Ireland, Irish missionaries in the sixth and seventh centuries set out to establish numerous Celtic monasteries in Britain. These monasteries extended all the way from Somerset's Glastonbury in the south of England, to the island of Lindisfarne in the North Sea. In such institutions the physical manifestations of the best that man could do, often represented by great art, was produced in the name of God as it was in Ireland. The elegant display script of the technically brilliant *Lindisfarne Gospels* is a glorious example of Irish virtuosity in seventh-century manuscript production in Britain. For a time some early English kings were sent for their education to Irish monastic schools. One of these kings, writes Peter Ellis, was Northumbria's Aldfrith, who wrote poetry in Irish and who also may have written *Beowulf*, the earliest epic poem written in English.

Britain Finally Christianized

By the seventh century the Irish or "Celtic" church, with assistance from Rome in some parts of the island, had spread Christianity throughout Britain, forever changing all phases of its culture. It was the monastic Celtic church, however, not the Roman church, that dominated Christianity in Britain and Ireland for four hundred years.

Irish Monasteries Internationally Renowned

The Irish monasteries of Iona in Scotland and Lindisfarne in England, among many others in Britain, became famous throughout Europe as great centers of learning, with Iona additionally acclaimed for both its political and ritual importance.

Iona: Burial Place Of Kings

In 563 A.D. Saint Columba had a choice of many places in which to found his Irish abbey, but with his followers he chose the ascetic way of life on rocky, windswept Iona. Located desolately among the Scottish Hebrides, exposed to all the furies of the northern Atlantic, it is only 3½ miles long and 1½ miles wide.

Yet it would consequently become internationally esteemed not only as a great center of learning, but as a final resting place for royalty. The cemetery of Saint Oran's church on the *holy* island of Iona contains not only the graves of almost *fifty* Scottish kings, but also ten kings of Ireland, Norway and France. It is here that the mortal remains of both

Macbeth and Duncan, whose memory is immortalized in Shakespeare's tragedy, *Macbeth*, are buried.

IRISH MISSIONARIES RETURN TO THE LANDS OF THEIR ANCESTORS

Saints And Scholars Of Ireland

The Irish were not content with Christianizing only the pagans of Britain. In 590 A.D. the Irish missionary Saint Columbanus, a younger contemporary of Saint Columba, bypassed Britain when he sailed with a symbolic twelve followers from Ireland to France, imbued with the zeal to convert pagans there to Christianity. His journey led the way for countless other Irishmen of his own and later generations who would similarly devote their lives to spreading learning and Christianity throughout much of Europe during medieval times. By the ninth century, Irish monks were internationally renowned for their learning, with Irish masters teaching at the courts of Charlemagne and other European nobility.

A Return To Their Roots

As Celts, the Irish missionaries traveling to continental Europe were returning to the original homeland of their people. But where their ancestors had once fought Germans and Romans with war chariot and spear, they set out now to conquer armed with knowledge and the word of God. The monasteries they established were spread through much of Germany, France, northern Italy, Switzerland, and Austria—all parts of what had once been the vast domain of the Celts.

Saint Columbanus

Also called *Columban*, this pioneering sixth-century Irishman was born in Ireland in 542 and studied for many years there at the monastery of Saint Comgall at Bangor and under the tutelage of Saint Sinell. He later established monastic retreats in France, including those at Luxeuil and Fountaine. He was eventually driven from Burgundy under threat of death by Queen Brunhilde when he refused to baptize the illegitimate child of a nobleman. Some of his surviving letters show him to have been an outspoken person apparently afraid of no one—even Pope Gregory the Great, with whom he disagreed about the dating of Easter. Some of his verse has also survived, including a boat song he wrote for his companions pulling their oars against the flow of the Rhine in Germany.

Legacy Of Saint Columbanus

France was only one of the countries in which Columbanus traveled and worked with his group of dedicated Irish followers. Today hundreds of organizations can trace their origins back to the institutions he started. He occupies a place of honor in the history of Frankish Germanic tribes, among whom he was known as *Kolumban*, well remembered by Germans today for having been a patron of art and culture, and credited with the flourishing of religious orders throughout the land. He established a monastery in what is now Switzerland at Bregenz on Lake Constance. Wherever he went he brought handwritten books, artistically styled and produced by Irish minds and hands nearly 1000 years before the fifteenth-century Gutenberg Bible would be printed with movable type in Mainz, Germany. In northern Italy in 612, Columbanus founded the monastery of Bobbio which would become famous and attract some of the greatest minds of Europe. The library of this institution grew to contain many hundreds of priceless manuscripts, some originals, some copies of originals. Many of the Latin texts at Bobbio were written by Irish monks who left marginal notes penned in the Irish or Gaelic language. While a majority of items were religious in nature, the library also included works by classical writers such as Horace, Virgil, Cicero, and Pliny the Elder. There were also texts on such subjects as music, grammar, and mathematics. During the ninth through the twelfth centuries it was an important center of European cultural life. The monastery later declined, and the invaluable manuscripts were dispersed in the fifteenth and sixteenth centuries. The monastery itself was dissolved in the early nineteenth century.

Saint Gall

The attractive university city of Saint Gallen in eastern Switzerland has the reputation of being "the cradle of Western culture." It was named after the Irish monk Saint Gall, who founded it in 612 A.D., and who is buried there. His simple monk's cell rapidly developed into a monastery which by the eighth century was already one of the most important cultural centers in the West. The craftsmen and peasants who settled in the "Villa Sancti Galli" outside the monastery walls formed the beginning of the present Saint Gallen which, with a population of 70,000, is the seventh largest city in Switzerland.

The monastery founded by Saint Gall had two schools, one for the laity, and one for those who had taken religious vows. Rhetoric and logic were taught among many other subjects. Students were punished if caught speaking anything but Latin. Today the Abbey Library of Saint Gallen is considered to be the most venerable national treasure of Switzerland. Its present building, constructed in 1758, has an elaborately ornate main hall which is considered to represent Switzerland's most beautiful rococo room. Unlike other institutions of its kind, the Saint Gall Abbey Library did not become a mere museum, but has remained a living library open to scholars and a fascinated public to the present time—a continuous existence of about 1,300 years, beginning centuries before the birth of the hero William Tell and the formation of Switzerland. The lives and works of Saint Gall and his followers, along twith *The Rules of Saint Columbanus*, are carefully preserved in the priceless, original manuscripts numbered 553, 560, 562, 564, 914, and 916 on display behind glass in the library. These include beautifully illuminated manuscripts written in the Irish language.

Pages of the priceless 750 A.D. book of the Irish missionary St. Gall on display in the Abbey Library of St. Gallen, the city this Irishman founded in the eighth century in the region of Europe which would eventually become Switzerland. The manuscript relates to the Scripture according to St. Mark. Photo courtesy Stiftsbibliothek, St. Gallen.

Traveling in Switzerland has become easier since the time of Saint Gall. To overcome the difficult terrain, a particular 375 kilometers of the Swiss rail system has no less than 500 bridges and 120 tunnels.

Saint Kilian

The seventh-century Irish missionary-monk Saint Kilian first visited the Main River of Germany and the area around Würzburg when it was still undeveloped and occupied by a tribal people who were totally "heathen." Along with Totnan and Kolonat, two fellow Irish monks, Kilian made a pilgrimage to Rome from where he received permission from the Pope in 687 to return to Würzburg as Apostolic Bishop of the country around the Main River, now known as Franconia. Totnan and Kolonat accompanied him back to Germany. Within two years Kilian and his companions had traveled throughout the country, "spreading the word of God, baptizing, and impressing the people with their religious fervor, purity of thought and selflessness." In 688 the local ruler was baptized and then ordered to dissolve his "improper" marriage to his wife, Geilana. In the ruler's absence in 689, Geilana had Kilian and his two fellow monks beheaded and their bodies buried. According to written records, both Geilana and the man who killed the monks became raving mad and "died horrible deaths." Miracles occurred at the place where Kilian and his companions had been buried, and subsequently in 752 their bones were disinterred and finally laid to rest with suitable ceremony in a place over which now stands the great four-spired Cathedral of Saint Kilian in the center of the university city of Würzburg. Thirteen hundred years later, Kilian the Irish monk and bishop is the patron saint of Franconia, with his holy day celebrated every July. His statues are prominently erected on a bridge leading into

Würzburg and, along with a separate, full-sized Celtic cross carved in stone, in the magnificent Marienberg Castle on the hill overlooking the city. In 1989 Würzburg held a four-month festival and exhibition at the castle to mark the thirteenth century since Kilian died in 689. At the same time, the German Post Office (die Deutsche Bundespost) issued a stamp commemorating the 1300th anniversary of the three Irish saints' martyrdom. It is coincidental that centuries before the birth of Saint Kilian, Würzburg was originally a Celtic settlement.

Statue of Saint Kilian, a seventh-century Irishman who is now the patron saint of Germany's Franconia. Seen here with a stone Celtic cross at the entrance to an exhibition in Würzburg's Marienberg Castle, marking the 13 centuries since Kilian converted the region to Christianity. Photo by author.

Saint Koloman

Of the Irish Celts in the Middle Ages who traveled back to the continental European lands of their ancestors, none presents a more unusual story than an Irishman named *Koloman*. In 1012 A.D., on his return to Ireland from a pilgrimage to Palestine in the Holy Land, he was arrested and accused of being a Slavic spy while he was passing through what is now Austria. There were various opposing factions in the area at the time, and with his strange speech and dress, the incarceration of Koloman must have seemed reasonable. He was tortured and ordered to confess, but he repeatedly refused to do so until, eventually, he was hanged on a barren holly tree along with two common robbers.

Local history says that the bodies of the two robbers quickly decomposed and were eaten by birds of prey. Koloman's body, however, did not decompose even after some months, and the previously dead holly tree sprouted leaves, an event judged to be a miracle by the local people. A church was built on the site in which Koloman's body was reverently buried. Three years later, Henry I of Austria had the still undecomposed body brought to the site of his royal residence in Melk. Koloman was proclaimed a saint by Pope Innocent IV on May 20, 1244. Today this Irishman is the patron saint of Austria, a place where, coincidentally, the first Celts worked as miners and traders nearly three thousand years earlier. Churches in Austria and in Germany's Bavaria are named in his honor. Melk draws people from many countries to its magnificent eighteenth-century Benedictine abbey built on the site centuries after Koloman was first buried there. The immense abbey high on its hill overlooking the River Danube is one of the most impressive baroque buildings in the world. Koloman's remains now finally rest in an elaborate side-altar in the cathedral-sized abbey church.

The Austrians could have given no greater honor to this medieval Irishman. They claim that Melk is where their country was born, and is subsequently called "the cradle of Austria." The abbey is the center of Melk, and the abbey church where Koloman lies is the center of the abbey.

Charlemagne And His Irish Scholars

The court of Charlemagne at Aachen was in its time the center of Europe's greatest intellectual activity. A Frankish king and ninth-century Emperor of the West, Charlemagne (742-814) attracted many Irish scholarly monks to his palace, including the astronomer Dicuil, whom he installed as teacher-in-residence. Another Latin-speaking Irish monk favored by the royal court was Johannes Scottus Eriugena, who would write the treatise, *De Divisione Naturae*, which has been called the first great philosophical work of Western Europe. Charlemagne established monastic schools for two other Irish scholars, one in France and the other in Italy.

Kings With Strange Names

Charlemagne (Charles the Great) was the son of *Pepin the Short*. Charles II, king of the West Franks, was named *Charles the Bald* (who had nothing to do with another Charles II, known as *Charles the Lame*, king of Naples). Charles III, king of the East Franks, is known to history as *Charles the Fat*. He should not be confused with another King Charles III who was named *Charles the Simple* (and who in turn was the son of Louis II, known as *Louis the Stammerer*). Charles VI was known as *Charles the Mad*. It became inevitable in modern times that the concept of royalty would be regarded as archaic, if not intellectually primitive.

History will decide what nickname may be given to Britain's present Prince Charles, who at the time of this writing was first in line to succeed his multi-billionaire mother to become Charles III, King of England, Wales, Scotland, and Northern Ireland. Charles' main requirement on being born to Elizabeth II was to marry a non-Catholic virgin who would produce an heir. Perhaps posterity will know him from the *Age of Tabloids* as Charles the Mate of Diana. History will show that, unlike his predecessors, this twentieth-century Charles did not have to make important decisions to exist.

A tenth-century king of England was named *Ethelred the Unready*. His problems as a weak king, regrettably for him, coincided with the time of the deadly Viking raids being made not only into England, but into Ireland, too.

11

Irish Celts Meet the Vikings, the Normans and the English

Ireland's Isolation Nears An End

By the eighth century the Anglo-Saxon warlords in Britain collectively controlled their eastern half of the island—to be called *England.* The rest of the country, including much of Scotland, Wales, and Cornwall, was still mainly occupied by the island's original, Celtic Britons.

Across the Irish Sea, Ireland continued in her Golden Age, a nation which for eight centuries had been invaded only by Christianity and the consequent knowledge of Latin and writing. The Irish were then in no immediate danger of invasion from the Anglo-Saxons who were still fighting among themselves and struggling to hold on to or increase the size of their various sections of eastern Britain.

Conditions in Britain and Ireland, however, would soon change dramatically with the appearance on the international scene of exceedingly aggressive, seaborne visitors from the north. Some of these would form the first unfriendly force to invade and forever change Ireland in her more than eight centuries of Celtic life.

From the end of the eighth century A.D., the farming, fishing and hunting peoples of the northern territories today known as Scandinavia grew restless and began to explore the world beyond their own—as seafaring *Vikings.* With their colorful attire and ships they are well documented in popular films and books. "Among the causes that drove the Vikings from their lands," says the *Columbia Encyclopedia*, "were overpopulation, internal dissension, quest for trade, and thirst for adventure." A hunger for plunder and new lands took them south along the coasts of many European countries including Britain, France and Italy, and west into Scotland and Ireland. They also went into what is now Russia where they founded the first Russian state. Their international incursions created a truly influential period of Scandinavian expansion from the ninth to the eleventh centuries A.D. Important enough in history to be called the *Viking Age*, it would change the faces of France, England and Ireland forever.

Who Were The Vikings?

Known by some as the *Danes*, the Vikings who invaded Ireland were as much from Norway and Sweden as from the region now called Denmark. Sometimes in intense competition with each other, they were also known as Norsemen or Northmen, and collectively nicknamed the *Sea Wolves*. Their high-prowed "longships" sat up to thirty oarsmen and could carry as many as ninety people. Square sails augmented the oars in favorable weather. When they began their European raiding, these Scandinavian people were the best shipbuilders and sailors in the world. They became dreaded throughout much of Europe because of the extreme ruthlessness of their seaborne raids.

The Sea Wolves In Ireland

The Vikings first struck Ireland in 795 A.D. Their visits in the years to come were noted for their extreme rapaciousness toward people and wanton destruction of property. Monasteries and homesteads alike were looted, burned, and their occupants slaughtered. Girls or women were sometimes spared only to be carried off with other booty for the pleasure of the raiders and for selling as slaves. The Irish *Annals of Ulster* recorded that in 820 A.D. Howth (near Dublin) was plundered and a large number of women taken as booty. An Irish historian of the time wrote of the "immense floods and countless sea-vomiting of ships of Danes...."

The *Annals* recorded various victories by the Irish in battle with the Vikings. But with Ireland divided into numerous, often feuding kingdoms, there was no organized national resistance to the invasions. Much the same situation existed in Anglo-Saxon Britain where the apparently invincible Vikings dominated much of what would one day be eastern England. It has been said that the Sea Wolves' reputation for ruthlessness often won battles for them before they even landed.

Career Plunderers

Beginning in the early ninth century, countless Viking warships brought to Ireland endless cargoes of Norsemen who, for generations, were actually career plunderers specializing in the raiding of foreign peoples whose lives and property were considered free for the taking. For these Scandinavians, it was a choice of staying back on the crowded farm (or fishing and hunting village), or going off as Vikings to see the world and make a fortune at the same time.

Essentially the Vikings would sail along exotic coasts with an exciting potential for miscellaneous, commercially viable loot, then go ashore where their fancy took them. Many a farmer in Britain or Ireland lost both his life and his daughter or wife on a Norseman's navigational whim.

Eighth-century Ireland had no towns or cities to plunder. The monasteries and the communities built around them were the next best thing, and these became favorite targets of the raiders. Often the priceless manuscripts found in them were burned, being of no use to the illiterate, pagan Norsemen. Instead they sought loot such as the secular treasures of kings which were often stored in monasteries. Desired loot included the valuable metal in religious and art objects. In 805 A.D., Vikings attacked the internationally renowned Irish abbey founded by Ireland's Saint Columba on Iona Island, Scotland, slaughtering its community of 68 monks. Some of the items carried off from Ireland's monasteries can today be seen in Scandinavian museums. The earliest surviving *crozier* or pastoral staff of an Irish Bishop (such as used by Saint Patrick) is in Stockholm, Sweden.

IRISH HEROES

No account of the Vikings and Ireland would be complete without mention of two Irish heroes who victoriously defended their island against the Vikings. One of them, named Mael Sechnaill, was a high king of Ireland in the early ninth century. He captured the Viking settlement on the River Liffey which would become the capital city of Dublin. He further established his authority by imposing a tithe on every Norse dwelling in the settlement.

The most famous of Irish heroes who fought the Vikings was also a high king of Ireland, Brian Boru. In 1014 A.D., at the battle of Clontarf just north of where Dublin now lies, his army decisively beat that of the "Danes." From that time on, Viking raiders encountered Celts in Ireland who effectively fought them off until the plundering finally ceased.

After years of pirating, some Norsemen from the northern cold began arriving in Ireland as permanent settlers. Their settlements along Ireland's coasts were the beginnings of the country's first towns, including Dublin, Limerick, Arklow, and Wexford. These more peaceful Norsemen established cooperative relationships and intermarried with the local people. In time these Celto-Scandinavians were absorbed into and became a part of the Irish population.

After the Vikings, the Normans would be the next foreigners to invade Ireland and add to its ethnic mix. They would not have to fight their way ashore. They came because the Irish king of Leinster, Dermot McMurrough, petitioned Henry II of England to send help to him in his feud with another Irish king. His action changed Irish history more than he could have ever imagined.

WHO WERE THOSE NORMANS?

To many people, Normandy and its beaches only mean that part of France through which World War II's Allied Forces began to invade Europe in June 6, 1944 (D-Day). Some of the American and British troops who fought their way ashore were unaware of the area's ancient history and of how Normandy acquired its name. At most they knew of it as a province of France chosen for the Allied invasion because its coast conveniently faced the English Channel.

The invasion's code name, "Operation Overlord," would have been historically appropriate for another invasion that occurred in the same place, but in the opposite direction nearly a thousand years earlier. It was a momentous event that would not only forever lead to changes in the societies of England and Ireland, but also their relationship with each other. Like all great historic occasions, it was preceded by previous, connecting events, in this case events involving the descendants of Vikings.

Some Vikings who never went to Ireland or Britain ended up in what is now Normandy in France—named after the

Norsemen themselves. There they mingled and became one with the indigenous population in what had once been a Celtic land.

How Vikings Became Normans

By the tenth century, the Vikings so dominated the Normandy coastal region that King Charles III of France made it a duchy and ceded it to them in 911 A.D. while investing the Viking chief, Rollo, as the first duke of Normandy. The Vikings abandoned piracy, accepted Christianity, and adopted the customs and language of France. The plural name "Norsemen" became *Normans*, and their territory, as a province of France, was named *Normandy*. They lost all connection with Scandinavia, but not their interest in travel and the acquisition of new lands, power, and wealth. It was an interest that would eventually take them into Ireland via Britain.

The man who was to become England's most important king was born in about 1026, the illegitimate son of Robert I, Duke of Normandy, and the young daughter of a lowly skin tanner. Sometimes called *William the Bastard*, he is better known as *William the Conqueror*. Born and raised in Normandy, France, he was destined to conquer England and become its ruler.

The Norman Conquest of Saxon England began with the Battle of Hastings in Kent, England. It was the most decisive battle in English history, and one of the most important in the history of western civilization. The bloody confrontation, lasting about eight hours, began and ended in a single day, October 14, 1066. Harold, King of England, led the English Saxons to defeat, and William, Duke of Normandy, led the Normans to victory.

The Normans won the battle despite having less fighting men. This was possible because their army was better trained and equipped. Stirrups were not yet used in England, and the Saxons thought that a horse was too unstable a platform from which to fight. William's cavalry, however, including his Celtic Bretons, stood securely in stirrups and used the weight of their charging horses to drive their lances home.

Harold Slain, His Body Mutilated

Various accounts tell of Harold's ghastly death at the Battle of Hastings. Apparently a group of Norman knights found the English king lying helplessly wounded. They slew him where he lay, then decapitated and further mutilated his body. It has been suggested that an ancient account of Harold's leg being cut off at the thigh is really a euphemism for cutting off the king's genitalia. If true, someone acquired a unique if grisly trophy. In any event, Harold's headless body was duly identified by his mistress with or without his genitalia.

A contingent of Breton (Celtic) warlords and their troops from Brittany made up about a third of William's victorious army. Ironically, many of these were probably descended from the Celts who sailed to France (Armorica) when driven out of Britain by the Anglo-Saxon invasion five centuries earlier. As a reward for their part in the successful conquest of England, William generously rewarded these Celtic supporters of his with lands he took from the vanquished Saxons—land that the Bretons' ancestors may well have once owned. Some of these French Celts settled in the west of Britain where their language was mutually understandable with that of the Celts still occupying Cornwall and Wales.

Most Famous Event In English History

The Norman Conquest of England has been described both as England's most devastating defeat, and as a critical element contributing to her future greatness. The celebrated Battle of Hastings was consequently one of the most important confrontations in history. William the Conqueror had the kind of dynamic characteristics that helped him make history and not just live it. Some modern English are proud to have him as a kind of symbolic ancestor, this man who conquered England, killed their beloved King Harold, and was the illegitimate son of a Viking warlord and a peasant girl of Gallic France who may have been of Celtic ancestry.

The Normans wasted no time in taking control of England. On Christmas Day, 1066, at London's Westminster Abbey, William, Duke of Normandy (today best known as William the Conqueror), was crowned William I, King of England. It was a perfectly legitimate kingship, even if the new king never did learn to speak English (or Anglo-Saxon). He had earned the right to sit on the throne of England the hard way and not by succession.

The Normans built castles and established their authority throughout much of Britain. William redistributed the ownership of English land, awarding vast tracts of it to his supporters and followers, including his Celtic military allies from Brittany. By 1087 only about eight per cent of the land was still owned by Anglo-Saxon aristocracy.

Under the Normans, England was unified politically, power was centralized, and feudalism introduced. Law, local government, learning, social organization, and religious administration (with Rome as its head) were all changed or adapted to Norman ways—representing influences that would be introduced to Ireland when Normans settled there permanently a hundred years later.

Origins Of The English Language

"Celtic" was the language of Britain for a millennium, the final 367 years of this period merging with the presence of the Roman conquerors of the island. The tongue that would be known as *English* began to develop from the language of the Angles and Saxons of northern Germany when they settled in eastern Britain following the fall of Rome. Invading Scandinavians of the Viking Age later added their linguistic influence to Britain. The final contribution to the English language after the Celts and the Vikings was from the Normans, whose French language came into being after Rome had introduced Latin to France's Gallic Celts—from which evolved the French language. With the Norman Conquest of England in 1066, the Norman French language, with its roots in a Romanized, Celtic land, further enriched the English language of the Angles and the Saxons in Britain and helped make it dominant among all the world's tongues.

Although still essentially a Germanic language, it has been suggested that without the Norman and other influences, English would otherwise today sound much like the Germanic language now known as Dutch.

The Painful Death Of William The Conqueror

In 1087, while riding in France, William received severe internal injuries when thrown from his horse. This harsh, unrelenting man, who had always appeared sternly unemotional, cried real tears when he later lay dying, praying for divine mercy while expressing penitence for the great slaughter that led to his exalted place in history. When approaching death, he was concerned about his possessions.

He wanted one of his sons to succeed him in ruling his vast Norman/French territories, and another son to separately succeed him as king of England, so that, by extension, these countries he had won in life would remain his in death. He died at dawn September 9, placing himself at the mercy of the Virgin Mary "by whose intercession," he is quoted as saying, "I may be reconciled to her Son our Lord Jesus Christ."

William Reappears Four Centuries After His Death

In a remarkable event, in 1522, Rome ordered that William the Conqueror's tomb be opened and his body examined. The 435-year-old embalmed king was found to be so extraordinarily well preserved that an artist was commissioned to paint his portrait. This painting hung on the tomb for some years until it disappeared without trace. Another painting, said to be a copy derived from the cadaverous original of 1522, can presently be seen in the church at Saint Etienne.

THE NORMANIZING OF IRELAND

Invasion By Invitation

The Romans and the Anglo-Saxon invaders of post-Roman Britain saw Ireland from a distance but never invaded her shores. Even the Normans, after conquering England, waited for a century before venturing into Ireland. And then they crossed the Irish Sea only on the invitation of an Irish king, Dermot McMurrough. That invitation in 1169 A.D. would have, for the Irish, the same, far-reaching consequences as the Battle of Hastings had for the English in 1066 A.D.

McMurrough, aware of the military prowess and superior fighting equipment of the Normans, wanted them to join forces with him in his fight with another Irish king. He went directly with his request to the court of Henry II, King of England. Henry agreed to help, allowing McMurrough to negotiate an arrangement with the Earl of Pembroke, a Norman aristocrat popularly known as *Strongbow.*

Strongbow's social importance and wealth, as with other aristocrats, were judged both by the number of people who looked on him as their lord, and by the size of his estate or estates. Like other nobles, Strongbow wished for more land than he already possessed. He saw McMurrough's invitation as an adventurous opportunity to acquire for himself an Irish domain unlimited in size by his English king.

Ireland in the twelfth century of Strongbow's time was divided by dynastic feuds. Its various leaders at first did nothing to stop the Normans' arrival in Ireland as long as it did not directly affect their own individual territories.

The Normans Become More Gael Than Gaul

Events went exceedingly well for Strongbow in Ireland. In time he captured Dublin, married an Irish princess (MacMurrough's daughter), and on his father-in-law's death, became king of Ireland's province of Leinster. Other Normans followed him and spread throughout Ireland, taking sides with some Irish chieftains to seize land from others. Eventually the Irish came to collectively recognize the Norman threat as a national one, and several battles ended in Norman defeats. But the well-armored Normans had come to stay in Ireland as they had in England. They built fine medieval castles, intermarried with the local people, and became more and more "Hibernicized." They adopted Irish dress, language, and custom to soon become, as in the popular saying: *Hibernicis ipsis Hiberniores* (more Irish than the Irish themselves).

Strongbow himself liked Ireland well enough to abandon his interests in Britain under King Henry II. Today his tomb lies in a place of honor in Christ Church Cathedral, Dublin. He led the way into Ireland for thousands of others of his kind, and represents, for the Irish, the exotic ancestral mix that William the Conqueror and his followers introduced to the English. One difference between them, however, was that while William I of England preferred to spend his time (and ultimately die) in once-Celtic France where he was born, Strongbow chose to live and die in Ireland.

English King Invades Ireland

In twelfth-century England, the Norman invaders had by definition become Anglo-Normans, and as such were becoming part of the "English." In 1171, Henry II of England grew worried about his share of the spoils from Ireland. He also worried about the independence and increasing "Irishness" of his nobles who had joined in the apparently good life across the Irish Sea—but had never bothered to return. He made a momentous decision and personally undertook an expedition into Ireland to consolidate the conquests that he liked to think had been made there in his name by Strongbow and other Anglo-Normans. This uninvited visit to Ireland by a English king and his army marked the beginning of London's centuries-long but ultimately futile attempt to subjugate its now part Scandinavian, part Norman, Celtic neighbor across the Irish Sea.

London would have possessive designs on Ireland for 800 years. Resistance from the Irish during this time has been historically referred to by the English as the "Irish problem"—a euphemism for a situation resulting directly from the perennial aggression of the English themselves. To the Irish, it could have been more accurately called the *English* problem.

Irish Clothes And Hairstyles Declared Illegal

Other English rulers after Henry II took extraordinary measures to stop the English who had gone to Ireland from being assimilated by the Irish. In 1366, the English-instituted "Statutes of Kilkenny" were enacted to prohibit "the English born in Ireland" from wearing Irish clothes and hair styles, and from speaking the Irish language—Gaelic, the language of Ireland and Scotland.

By the fifteenth century, the only part of the island controlled by the English was Dublin City and a small area around it called the *pale*. To the English, those inside the pale were under their control. Two centuries after Ireland's first invasion from England, Dublin and its pale was all that was under English control. Places and people "beyond the pale" were not. By the sixteenth century London would attempt to take all of Ireland.

Henry VIII Calls Himself King Of Ireland

In 1541 Henry VIII, King of England, arbitrarily gave himself the additional title, King of Ireland, and declared that his realms, including Catholic Ireland, were Protestant. He named himself head of the Church of England, and also proclaimed himself head of the Irish (Catholic) Church. He summarily beheaded those who offended him. To further flex his godlike power, he proclaimed that the titles of all lands in Ireland were to be withdrawn and re-granted.

The First Queen Elizabeth

On succeeding to the throne of England, Henry VIII's daughter, Elizabeth I, continued her father's arrogance toward Ireland, systematically trying to subjugate and even destroy the Irish as would many of the English who came after her. Elizabeth had known violence all her life. Her own mother, Anne Boleyn, one of Henry VIII's many wives, had her head hacked off with the approval of her father, a fact that did not deter Elizabeth from dutifully continuing her father's extreme disregard for the rights of others, sometimes to the point of absurdity. During her reign a law was passed prohibiting anybody in Ireland from wearing Irish-style clothing.

The men who applied the philosophy of Henry VIII's daughter had unlimited license to implement it to their every personal whim. Under her rule, English soldiers were repeatedly turned loose in the Irish countryside to pillage and murder at will, with no possibility of a human rights or international court of inquiry to follow.

English Headhunters

In his book, *Ireland, A History* (Weidenfeld and Nicolson London, 1980) Robert Kee presents various documented examples of the atrocious behavior of the English against the Irish in Ireland. He quotes from a sixteenth-century Englishman, Sir Humphrey Gilbert, who wrote describing one of Elizabeth's military representatives in Ireland who made a practice of having his men cut off heads of the Irish killed each day and brought back to his camp. There he had the heads set up on each side of the path leading to his tent. In this way, Sir Humphrey wrote, the Irish who were obliged to visit him were forced to see "...the heads of their dead fathers, brothers, children, kinsfolk and friends lie on the ground before their faces ..."

Elizabeth's measures against Catholics and others grew harsher during her forty-five-year reign (1558-1603). She imprisoned a possible competitor, the Catholic Mary Queen of Scots, for nineteen years before having her beheaded. Five years before her own death, when complaining about the amount of money being spent on trying to subjugate the people of Ireland, she presented for history the following statement (referring to the Irish who were defending their country from the marauding English):

> "We will not," she exclaimed, "suffer our subjects (the English) any longer to be oppressed by those vile rebels..."

A Top Career Woman Four Hundred Years Ago

Successful in her own country as a queen, Elizabeth I never married, although she had many suitors. She gave her friend, Sir Walter Raleigh, 42,000 acres of land taken from Irish farmers. She also gave him a charter to found a colony in the New World. In return, Raleigh named his American colony *Virginia* after his so-called "Virgin Queen."

Elizabeth never knew Ireland (or Virginia) from personal experience, but by the time of her death in 1603, she had, through the men of her military forces, systematically devastated much of the island and many of its inhabitants. The brutality and killing by the English (politically the *British* after 1707) in Ireland went on for centuries more after Elizabeth's death. The following paragraphs represent some events occurring in just a part of the seventeenth century.

Irish Parliament Elected: Opposes Penal Laws

In Ireland's Kilkenny, in 1642, Irish leaders met and elected a national parliament within an *Irish Confederacy*.

They demanded a repeal of the English-made Penal Laws designed to exclude Catholics in Ireland from civil life by forbidding them to buy or inherit land, build churches, or to attend their church.

The Adventurers' Act

The Adventurers' Act of 1642 was enacted in London to invite wealthy individuals among the English to "adventure" or invest their money towards the violent conquest of the Irish people. Instead of expecting to make a direct money profit, however, the investors in this capitalist plan were to be rewarded with land taken from the Irish. The more money one invested, the bigger and better the exotic estate one hoped to get across the sea in Ireland. It was one way that Ireland acquired many rich, absentee landlords—and many landless Irish farmers.

In 1645 a treaty was signed between the Irish Confederacy and the royalist English government which included the repeal of the hated Penal Laws and a halt to all further colonization by the English in Ireland. But the treaty was soon made meaningless by the English when they violently changed their leadership.

In 1649 the English executed their monarch, Charles I, declaring the kingship as "unnecessary and burdensome to the public interests of the people." Oliver Cromwell, a leader of the Puritan cause, was personally vociferous in demanding the king's execution. On Charles' death, Cromwell was named Lord Protector of England. He also assumed the title of Commander-in-Chief *and* Lord Lieutenant of Ireland. He was to blatantly ignore the 1645 treaty England had signed with Ireland.

Cromwellian "Conquest" Of Ireland

Today many see Cromwell as an extreme bigot with a violent intolerance toward those who did not fit in with his view of how the world should be. History knows him for the ruthlessness of an expedition he personally led into Ireland in 1649 which began with the massacre of much of the population of the city of Drogheda, including the English (but incorrectly Catholic) commander, Sir Arthur Aston, who was beaten to death by his fellow Englishmen.

Estimating that he had killed about two thousand men in Drogheda, including English royalist officers, Cromwell wrote after the massacre that "all this was done by the Spirit of God: and therefore it is right that God alone should have all the Glory."

A more realistic estimate is that Cromwell and his soldiers killed about 3,500 men, women and children during a two-day rampage in Drogheda. Another massacre occurred with Cromwell's troops slaughtering about 2,000 women and children in the city of Wexford. The death of 5,000 more people were attributed to the English ruler's attack on the city of Limerick. Cromwell's army in Ireland consisted of at least 22,000 men. Their weaponry, including siege artillery and heavy field guns, was superior to anything possessed by Irish patriots.

The deliberate destruction of the Irish nation's food was a part of Cromwell's plan. Additional "military" weapons made available to the English soldiers included quantities of scythes and sickles used for wasting Irish crops in the field before they could be harvested. Other crops were burned, and cattle were killed in great numbers.

Irish Population Depleted By A Half-Million

By 1652 the Physician-General to the English army in Ireland, William Petty, reported that "...about 504,000 of the Irish perished and were wasted by sword, plague, famine, hardships and banishment between the 23rd of October, 1641, and the same day in 1652." This represents the deaths of more than a third of the Irish people at that time—which suited those English who coveted Irish land.

To Hell Or Connaught

Following the Cromwellian conquest, after Ireland had been bludgeoned into apparent submission, the English decided to take the best Irish land by banishing surviving Irish farmers to the barren province of Connaught west of the Shannon river (where rock is almost more common than soil). Backed up by their large and well-equipped army, the English ordered the Irish farmers "to Hell or Connaught." It was just a part of English aggression towards their smaller neighbor which would continue into the twentieth century.

By any measure it was a poor return for the Celtic island nation that had once sent its missionary monks to spread literacy and Christianity into pagan, Anglo-Saxon Britain.

12

Celtic Legacy in American History

The Last Great Celtic Migration

The ancient Celts migrated and settled throughout much of Europe during the first seven centuries of their existence beginning in about 750 B.C. Before developing the necessary boatbuilding and seafaring technology to reach and settle the islands of Britain and Ireland, they were farmers, artisans, and creators of original art throughout much of continental Europe. Alexander the Great knew the Celts first hand in Bulgaria in 355 B.C., just as Julius Caesar would two hundred years later in Italy, Switzerland, France and Britain.

That was more than two millennia ago. By the time of the European colonizing of North America, it seemed natural that Celtic Ireland, being the closest part of the "Old World" to the "New World," should provide proportionately the greatest number of immigrants, and it did. Some Celtic immigrants were driven by famine, some by religious, economic, and political persecution from the English. Yet others sailed across the Atlantic acting on the Celtic penchant for exploration and adventure that had taken their ancestors across uncharted seas from mainland Europe to populate Britain and Ireland.

Many Celtic immigrants to America were Welsh—so many that in Pennsylvania they once published books in the Welsh (Celtic) language for use in their American community. Many Celts emigrated not just to America, but also to Canada where Scottish place names such as Nova Scotia (New Scotland), Kirkwall, Stromness and Scapa can be found today. Gaelic is still spoken in parts of Cape Breton, a place where visitors can stay at the magnificent *Keltic Lodge*, described as Nova Scotia's flagship resort. Descendants of Scottish Highland settlers at Saint Ann's keep the old ways alive at the Gaelic College with annual Highland games. Radio stations in Newfoundland regularly play Irish music and feature Irish singers to audiences of predominantly Irish descent. On Newfoundland's rugged coast lies Cape Spear, the wave-lashed, easternmost tip of the north American continent. Its rocky finger points dramatically across the Atlantic over which Celtic immigrants from Scotland, Wales and Ireland came to the New World with their hopes and dreams, many of them to escape the practices of those who ruled from London.

Many Americans who mark their national independence on July 4 are not aware of a third stanza of the American National Anthem which was diplomatically removed during World War II. This stanza, paying tribute to those who valiantly fought for freedom from the British, included the words:

> "...foul footsteps' pollution of the British
> o'er the land of the free and the home of the brave."

The American Revolution of 1775 to 1783 involved many patriots of Celtic heritage. The historic figures who signed the American Declaration of Independence in 1776 included three men who were born in Ireland, two who were born in Scotland, and two born in Wales. Ten other signers were of Irish, Scottish or Welsh descent, including John Hancock whose family came from Ireland. Thomas Jefferson, of Welsh ancestry, drafted the document itself. Irish-born Charles Thomson made the first finished copy of the document, and

John Dunlap, also born in Ireland, first printed it. An Irishman, architect James Hoban, born in Kilkenny, Ireland, designed and built the White House—and rebuilt it after it was burned by the British in 1814. (Eventually thirteen United States Presidents could claim Irish ancestry, including William McKinley, Ulysses S. Grant, and Ronald Reagan. Three presidents were born from parents who came directly form Ireland, including James Buchanan and Andrew Jackson.)

During the American Revolution, the ill-fated commander-in-chief of the British forces, Sir Henry Clinton, said that the best soldiers among the American rebels were the Irish (and hopefully proposed augmenting his own demoralized army with some of them). In 1784, after the successful Revolution, a speaker in the "Irish" parliament of then British-occupied Ireland lamented that "America was lost by Irish emigrants." A hundred years later, with so many Irishmen in America, a British home secretary petulantly complained that the rebellious Irish were now out of reach of the British government.

During the Revolution, Irish-American John Sullivan was a lawyer who served as one of George Washington's most able generals. Promoted to major general for his military successes against the British, he was later elected as New Hampshire's first governor and was influential in getting the Constitution ratified. As many as fifteen of Washington's top officers were born in Ireland. Not all the Celts who fought against the British in America were Irish. Scottish-born Alexander McDougall, a fiery opponent to British trade restrictions in America, was a founder of the *Sons of Liberty* organization in New York. He served in the army against the British throughout the Revolution and was later in charge of West Point.

An Irish American won honors for the Revolution at sea. John Barry was born in Wexford, Ireland. In 1776, while commanding the American brig, *Lexington*, he captured the British tender *Edward*, the first British ship taken by a commissioned American ship. In 1782 he took two other British vessels after a fight. Barry has been called the father of the American Navy.

The "modern" Celtic migration was not confined to America. By 1851 in Australia, for example, 30% or more of the Europeans who settled that land were from Ireland, albeit involuntarily for some of them. (The 1990's Prime Minister Keating was of Irish descent.) Yet even allowing for the thousands of Celts who went to Australia and New Zealand, the journeying to North America from Europe was to be the last great Celtic migration in the world. While Scotland and Wales contributed significantly to the European settlement of America, the largest number of Celts who emigrated to America, however, was from Ireland—about 5 million in 150 years (more than the average annual population of Ireland itself).

The early immigrant vessels to America were called "coffin ships" because four passengers, men and women together, slept in a space six by eight feet. The ships could also have been given this name for their ever-recurring outbreaks of cholera and typhoid. A further danger lay in the unseaworthiness of the ships themselves. Some of them sailed into the stormy Atlantic with their desperate but hopeful passengers and were never seen again. The approximate location of at least one doomed ship, the *Ocean Monarch*, is known. It burned and sank with a loss of 186 lives when still within sight of Liverpool, its port of embarkation.

Once at sea, exploitive captains and crews sold spoiled food to the passengers at extortion prices. Fresh drinking water sometimes ran out before reaching New York. A thousand steerage passengers were crowded onto the bigger ships, but only the privileged few in cabin class were allowed to enjoy the fresh air on the open decks.

Gallows Instead Of Statue Of Liberty

Immigrants arriving in New York before 1886 were not greeted by the Statue of Liberty holding her lamp beside the Golden Door. The place where the statue would stand was then known as Bedloe's Island, a littered, desolate place with a military prison and a still-standing gallows to greet the newcomers. Yet for many Celts from Britain and Ireland, life in America offered freedom and opportunities infinitely more attainable than under English rule.

Americans associated with Celtic homelands who achieved fame include such diverse figures as John F. Kennedy, 35th president of the United States; Scottish-born Alexander Graham Bell who invented the telephone; automobile pioneer and industrialist giant, Henry Ford, (whose grandfather was an immigrant from a tenant farm in Ireland's County Cork); Scottish-born Andrew Carnegie, son of a weaver, who became a giant among industrialists, mainly in steel; Welsh-born Samuel Milton Jones who made a fortune as an inventor and industrialist in the oil business and is remembered as a reformer who introduced a minimum wage and an 8-hour day for his workers; George M. Cohan who between 1901 and 1940 wrote and produced 80 Broadway plays and musical reviews in which he often performed (his Irish grandparents changed their name from O'Caomhan to the more easily pronounced Cohan on emigrating to America). Ronald Reagan, two-term president of the United States, is a more recent example of a Celt who made it to the top. During his presidency, Irish-named Brian Mulroney, simultaneously served as Canada's leader. While on an official visit to Ireland in 1995, President Clinton of the United States hoped to meet Irish relatives (his mother's maiden name was Cassidy). He was just one among millions of Americans with a similar ancestral background.

Immigrants to America shared the dream of a new and better life. Most of them found it, however anonymously. A select number of immigrants or their descendants accumulated multi-million dollar fortunes. Others found fame. Some achieved both. All immigrants, Celtic or non-Celtic, rich or poor, contributed to making the United States the greatest nation on earth.

Too numerous to more fully list here, the Irish or their descendants who became rich in America would have town-houses and lavish country estates to match their fortunes. Some typical names include the Murrays, McDonalds, Cuddihys, Cooleys, Murphys, Hennessys, Conniffs, Sullivans, MacGuires, Dohenys, O'Briens, Floods, and Mackays, to mention just a few. They married nationally and internationally into other "monied" families, both fellow "rich Irish" and others. Anne McDonnell, the direct descendant of a poor Irish immigrant, married, in America's "Wedding of the Century," Henry Ford II, grandson of industrialist Henry Ford (whose own grandfather was Irish-born as noted above). Anne McDonnell Ford's daughter, Charlotte Ford, married Greek shipping tycoon Stavros Niarchos. Another daughter married an Italian relative of the Rothchilds. A cousin married into the Mellons, still one of the extremely rich Irish-American families in the U.S. today. Another Irish-American married one of the Dutch-American Vanderbilts of financial fame. Yet another union of two wealthy Irish American families occurred in the marriage between Joseph Bradley Murray and Mary Teresa Farrell, daughter of the "Steel King," James A. Farrell, head of both the United States Steel Company and the Farrell Steamship

Line. John B. Kelly of Philadelphia not only made himself wealthy, but also fathered the beautiful Grace Kelly who romanced Gary Cooper and Clark Gable on the screen before becoming a real princess by marrying Prince Rainier of Monaco. The Buckley family is another that made it into the big league, with the original Will Buckley leaving a fortune estimated to exceed $100 million. One son, James, was elected U.S. senator. Another is William F. Buckley, Jr., author, editor of the conservative *National Review* magazine, essayist, lecturer, and television personality.

Irish Americans who achieved fame, if not great wealth, include the writers F. Scott Fitzgerald, John O'Hara, and playwright Eugene O'Neill—who was awarded the Nobel prize in literature. World renowned film stars of Irish descent include Spencer Tracy, James Cagney and John Wayne. Film director John Ford (born Sean O'Feeney, the son of Irish immigrants) in 1914 started out his adult life traveling when only eighteen years old from Boston to Hollywood in search of a career. Within three years, by age 22, he had become so skilled at directing motion picture films that he was signed up by Universal Studios from where he went on to direct over 80 films and win four Academy Awards. His films (which made stars of Henry Fonda, Katherine Hepburn and John Wayne, among many others) include such classics as *The Informer*, *The Grapes of Wrath*, *Stagecoach*, *Young Mr. Lincoln*, *How Green Was My Valley* and *The Quiet Man*. In 1973 the President of the United States presented him with the Medal of Freedom, the country's highest civilian award.

The following are a few examples of people with an Irish connection who made a considerable mark in the New World, but who are not generally known.

Charles Carroll Of Carrollton: Signer Of The Declaration Of Independence

The grandfather of Charles Carroll, descended from an old and noble Catholic Irish family, came to Maryland in 1688 as a lawyer. By the time his son was grown in the 1700's, Maryland's Protestants had made it illegal for Catholics to vote or to hold public office, or for Catholic lawyers to practice. By then, however, the land-owning and business-oriented Carrolls were the wealthiest people in Maryland—some said in all the colonies. The third-generation Charles Carroll—the one who would later sign the American Declaration of Independence—was sent by his wealthy parents to school for 16 years in Europe (ten years in France, and six years in London studying law in the Temple). He returned to Maryland in 1765 when his father gave him a ten-thousand-acre spread of his own in Frederick County, which would be called Carrollton. In 1768 he married Mary Darnall. With religious discrimination diminished, he was nominated for Congress, but chose not to serve. He accepted a second nomination because he thought it his duty. He had come to be considered Maryland's "First Citizen" by the time he signed the Declaration of Independence in 1776. When he resigned from the Maryland Senate in 1792, he owned over seventy thousand acres in Maryland, Pennsylvania and New York. Yet, in his old age he became famous, not as the richest man in the country, but as the only surviving signer of the American Declaration of Independence. He had seen George Washington, John Adams, and Thomas Jefferson come and go as presidents. People wanted the privilege and honor of seeing the only man alive who had been a *signer*. He died at age 95 in the year 1832, a distinguished American who happened to be a member of one of the earliest Irish American families.

George Berkeley (1685-1753)

Once the Bishop of Cloyne in Ireland's County Cork, Dublin-educated Berkeley is best known in history as a philosopher and for his original contributions to the world's philosophic thought. In addition to giving his name to the main campus of the University of California, he advised on the foundation of both Columbia University, New York, and the University of Pennsylvania. He donated his main library to Harvard, and also gave 1,000 books to Yale.

John Mackay

Born poor in 1831 in Dublin, Ireland, John Mackay emigrated at age nine to America, where he made his first fortune mining in Nevada before moving to New York. He would also maintain lavish homes in London and Paris. In London, Queen Victoria received his Irish-American wife, Louise, and the Prince and Princess of Wales dined at the Mackays' home, an event of which Louise would later say that the prince, who by custom had the right to approve the menu in advance, suggested "neither additions or subtractions." The Prince of Wales was charmed by John Mackay's gentle manners, calling him "the most unassuming American I have ever met." Two members of Mackay's family would later marry titled Europeans, occurrences which displeased him. In New York in 1883, Mackay formed the Commercial Cable Company and won a long legal battle against the Western Union telegraph monopoly. The company Mackay formed, whose ships would lay cables across the Pacific and Atlantic oceans, was the first to combine cable, radio, and telegraphic services under one management (Western Union bought the company in 1943). When he died in 1902 it was said that Mackay didn't know to within 20 millions what he was worth. His son Clarence Mackay and his wife in the 1920's gave a famous ball on their immense (six-hundred-acre) Long Island estate for yet another Prince of Wales (the future Duke of Windsor and King of England). Mackay's granddaughter, Ellin, married America's favorite composer, Irving Berlin, who fathered her three daughters. It was for Ellin that Irving Berlin wrote one of his most enduring songs, "Always."

Richard O'Neill, Sr.

In 1882, a 57-year-old Irishman named Richard O'Neill went shopping for 227,000 acres of prime grazing land sprawling across the vast areas now known as Southern California's Orange and San Diego Counties. He ultimately acquired the immense ranch he sought in the face of odds which would have daunted ordinary men. To make the transaction possible, he secured the financial backing of fellow Irish immigrant James Flood, the "Silver King of Nevada," who had astutely cornered the stock market on the Comstock Lode, America's most famous silver mine. The two men, who had known each other in San Francisco, became equal partners on a handshake, with O'Neill to work off his half at five hundred dollars a month as resident manager of the huge property, which by 1923 would grow to 230,000 acres and be consolidated under the name "The Santa Margarita Co." In 1939 the ranch was divided between descendants of the two families, with the O'Neills taking the Orange County part, while the Floods took the lower portion in San Diego County (part of which in 1942 became the United States Marine Corps' Camp Pendleton, the largest training base of its kind in the world). To help maintain their giant ranch in the mid-1960's, O'Neill's descendants developed a part of it into the planned 10,000-acre community which is today's modern city of Mission Viejo, home to over 86,000 people. The O'Neill family more recently also began the development of Rancho Santa Margarita, another planned community which, although not scheduled for completion until after the year 2000, is already home to more than 20,000 residents. In addition to leasing involvements which include farming, mining, and aerospace, the family still owns and operates the 40,000-acre Rancho Mission Viejo, the largest cattle operation in Southern California. The O'Neills' civic commitments include generous land donations for roads, schools, and parks. Today the family, including the present Richard O'Neill, Alice O'Neill Avery, and her son, Anthony Moiso (great-grandson of Richard O'Neill), continues to manage its vast holdings, making them, with a family wealth estimated at $500 million by *Forbes* magazine in 1992, a major force in Southern California. Like Henry Ford's grandfather, Richard O'Neill, Sr., was from County Cork in Ireland.

Thomas E. Murray

A second-generation Irishman, Thomas E. Murray was born in Albany, New York, in 1860, one of a carpenter's twelve children. His father died when he was nine and he left school to work as a city lamplighter to help support his mother and his siblings. With the little money he could save he put himself through two years of night school. He furthered his education by working for local architects and engineers and as an apprentice machinist. Specializing in the electrical field, he began to successfully invent and patent components and equipment at an early age, and had thus made himself a fortune worth more than ten million dollars by the time of his death in 1929. He finally held some thousand patents, a record exceeded only by his friend Thomas Edison. It has been said that while Edison invented the showy light bulb which everybody can see and appreciate (and that deservedly helped to make him famous), Thomas E. Murray invented many of the behind-the-scenes items which helped to provide the electrical current that lit the bulb.

Ed Doheny, Oil Baron

The son of an Irish immigrant, Edward Laurence Doheny was born in 1856, in Wisconsin. He learned about mining and prospecting while wandering through Texas, Arizona, and New Mexico. In 1892, at age 36, he was visiting the dusty, still undeveloped city of Los Angeles when he saw a man driving a wagon loaded with "*brea*" (Spanish for tar or pitch). He soon found that the stuff oozed naturally to the surface at the edge of town at a placed called Hancock Park. Local poor people used it as a kind of cooking and heating fuel. From his prospecting experience in the south, Doheny recognized it as crude oil. He quickly leased the land and brought in a gusher, the first of many he would eventually develop in the state. Within a few years he virtually controlled the oil production of California. He leased over a million acres in Mexico and developed a separate, highly profitable oil company there. In 1925 he was said to be the richest man in America, his personal fortune being worth more than a hundred million dollars, which would be worth the equivalent of billions, if calculated at the time of writing this book. In the late 1920's the Dohenys, by then including five grand-children—Lucy, Edward III, William, Patrick, and Timothy—built the majestic Tudor-style mansion called *Greystone* which, with its nineteen landscaped acres, is now a Beverly Hills city park and considered to be an architectural crown jewel in a landscape of fabled homes. The Dohenys required a house staff of fifteen and a grounds staff of twenty when they occupied the mansion. Greystone did not include the family's 410-acre Doheny ranch which would eventually be sold to become the Trousdale Estates, future location of many of Beverly Hills' grandest homes. In her time, Doheny's wife Estelle, while reigning as queen of her family's estate, was made a Papal countess—formally the Countess Estelle Doheny. Her husband remembered the land of his fathers by contributing to the Irish Freedom Movement. His descendants presently maintain branches of the family in such places as Washington, Hawaii, and especially in Beverly Hills, where the Irish American name of Doheny continues undiminished as a considerable social and economic presence. To honor this eminent family, a thoroughfare named Doheny Drive runs between Beverly Hills and adjoining Los Angeles, a city of which another Irish American, Richard Riordan, an attorney and highly successful businessman (coincidentally also said to be worth at least 100 million), was elected mayor by popular vote 101 years after Ed Doheny discovered oil there. But only Ed Doheny was immortalized by the Beach Boys when they included California's *Doheny Beach* (named after Ed Doheny) in the lyrics of their famous song, *Surfin' USA*.

William Mulholland

On November 4, 1913, forty thousand residents of Los Angeles, California, came to the San Fernando Valley just north of the city to witness the historic first arrival of water via a newly constructed aqueduct masterminded by the engineering genius of William Mulholland, an Irish immigrant. His project, an aqueduct carrying water hundreds of miles from northern California to the virtual desert on which Los Angeles and its surrounding communities would be built, was America's second largest engineering project, exceeded only by the Panama Canal which was being built at about the same time. Generations later Los Angeles' citizens take their water for granted. William Mulholland, known in his time as a hero who built Los Angeles, is remembered by the twenty-two-mile highway bearing his name which runs along the crest of the Santa Monica Mountains with spectacular views of the vast lands below he was directly responsible for bringing to life.

Celts in America over three centuries became involved in most areas of business and industrial endeavor. Many among them excelled in economic activities which included oil, steel, shipping, publishing, real estate, engineering, banking, and insurance. Of the current success stories, none is more extraordinary than that of an Irish American who worked his way to the top of the pizza business.

Thomas S. Monaghan

Born in 1937 in Ann Arbor, Michigan, Thomas (Tom) Monaghan, whose father died four years after his birth, spent his childhood in foster homes and orphanages. Following an honorable discharge from the U.S. Marine Corps, he held three part-time jobs to support himself at college. In 1960, at age 23, he and his brother James bought a small pizza store in Ypsilanti, Michigan, using part of a borrowed $900 as down payment. Within a year Tom traded James a Volkswagen for his share of the business. In 1965 he was sole owner of a small chain of pizza stores which he named "Domino's Pizza, Inc." By 1988, Domino's Pizza had 4,893 stores worldwide, including the U.S., Canada, Australia, Japan, Germany, and Hong Kong. Approximately two new stores are opened each day at the current rate of expansion, with a projection of 10,000 stores for the 1990's. Domino's is the world's largest pizza delivery company, accounting for more than half of the pizza delivered in the United States. Today, Thomas S. Monaghan is chairman of the board of Domino's Pizza, whose corporate headquarters are on Domino's Farms, a $250 million, 300-acre complex in Ann Arbor. Domino's Pizza had 1988 sales of $2.3 billion. Monaghan lives in Ann Arbor with his wife of twenty-eight years, Marjorie, whom he first met while delivering a pizza.

During the preparation of this book, people with Irish names headed such corporate giants as Reynolds Metals (annual sales $6.1 billion), Sears Roebuck ($53.8 billion), Capital Cities/ABC TV (sold in 1996 by its chairman, Thomas Murphy, to The Walt Disney Company for $19 billion), Union Carbide ($8.7 billion), and McDonald's ($6.1 billion). The CEO of Aluminum Co. of America, Paul H. O'Neill, modestly thanks "a little Irish luck" for his success at being the head of a corporation with annual sales of $10.9 billion. In Atlanta, Georgia, Irish American Donald Keough is president of Coca Cola (annual sales: $9 billion). Another *Fortune* 500 member, Irish-born, Jesuit-educated Anthony J. F. O'Reilly, is chairman of the Pittsburgh, Pennsylvania-based American corporate giant, H. J. Heinz (annual sales $6.7 billion). As its chief executive officer, Tony O'Reilly has been paid, in a single year, $57 million in salary, bonuses and stock options—more than any other CEO in America. In Ireland he owns a 500-acre estate and an impressive personal fortune with interests that include oil and Waterford crystal. As chairman and largest stockholder of Ireland's Independent Newspapers PLC, he is a press baron who controls 57% of all newspapers read every day in his native land. A horse lover, he regularly attends the Heinz 57 horse race in Ireland. He jokes that it would be almost unpatriotic for an Irishman not to own horses.

In the field of law, William Brennan, Jr., the son of Irish immigrants, served for thirty-four years as a member of the Supreme Court. It was said of him that no other justice had a more profound and sustained impact on public policy in the

United States. A champion of the underdog, the Harvard-educated Brennan was renowned for relentlessly seeking to uphold individual rights and to dispense equal justice under the law. On his retirement in 1990, the *Los Angeles Times*, typical of newspapers across the country, described him as "a towering figure in the history of American jurisprudence. The force and elegance of his landmark opinions...have made him one of the twentieth century's most influential Americans."

Americans of Celtic heritage, both those who achieved great success and the millions who did not, do not always have names obviously connecting them with the Celtic country of their origin. Some Celtic names, however, are more recognizable than others.

The Origin Of "Mac," "O" And "Fitz"

In North America and elsewhere, many people of Celtic descent have prefixes to their names, the origin and meaning of which they may not be aware. It is, for instance, widely but erroneously believed outside Ireland that the prefix "Mac" or "Mc" before a name makes it essentially Scottish. The Irish, however, while aware that there are indeed many Macs in Scotland, know that some of the commonest Irish names begin with Mac, with such examples as MacCarthy, MacDermot, MacGrath, MacGuinness, MacKenna, MacMahon, and MacNamara. Scotland is so close to Ireland that it is visible from that island's northern coast. Many names, with or without "Mac," are identical in both places. Scottish writer, Arthur Conan Doyle (Sir Arthur *Ignatius* Conan Doyle), was born of Irish parents, and has one of Ireland's most common names. Scotland historically took its name from the seafaring Irish *Scotti* (Latin *Scotia*) who originally settled it from Ireland. A *Gael* is an Irish person.

The Celtic language he or she may speak is called *Gaelic*, just as it is in Scotland.

Many names in Ireland and Scotland are variations of Scandinavian names brought by the Norsemen who mingled with the Celts a thousand years ago. The Irish name of McDowell, the name of this writer's maternal grandfather, is also known as *MacDougall* in Scotland's Hebrides Islands, the natural steppingstones between Scandinavia and Ireland. The original McDowell who gave his name to this Irish family was probably a Norseman who settled in Ireland before the Normans, according to Edward Lysaght in his book, *Irish Families*, an excellent source of information on the subject of Irish names.

Originally, the prefix "Mac" or "Mc" meant son (or son of). Somewhere back in time, for instance, there was once a man called *Mahon* whose son came to be called McMahon, meaning son of Mahon. As a footnote to history, the president of France from 1873-1880 was named Patrice MacMahon, the descendant of an Irish family of MacMahons who fled to France from British-occupied Ireland. (As a further footnote to Irish-French history, it was an eighteenth-century Irishman, Richard Hennessy, who founded France's world famous Hennessy brandy distillery.)

The "O" preceding an Irish name means grandson or male descendant. A name such as O'Connor thus originally meant that its owner was the grandson or descendant of a grandfather or other ancestor called Connor.

The prefix "Fitz" was brought to Ireland by the Normans. Like the prefixes "Mac" and "O," Fitz meant "descendant of." The first use of the name Fitzpatrick literally meant the descendant of somebody called Patrick. After centuries of intermarriage, the prefix has become a part of Irish culture, with no conscious Norman connotation among the general populations of either Ireland or America, a place where the line between *being* Celtic and *celebrating* the Celts is blurred at least once a year.

Saint Patrick's Day

The United States' population presently includes about forty million Americans descended from Irish immigrants. A good-natured expression of this presence is seen in the Saint Patrick's Day celebrations held each year on March 17, a date when countless citizens across the country, Irish or not, choose to wear "something green." It is said that New York City's annual Saint Patrick's Day parade had its humble beginnings in 1762. It has been growing bigger and better ever since. Its 228th parade in 1989, brought out 150,000 marchers and two million spectators along the route. Despite rain on the same date, nearly a half million lined the Chicago Saint Patrick's Day parade with its two hundred floats and marching units, including Yiddish and Italian groups. The Chicago River was made to run green for the day. In Savannah, Georgia, 250,000 people turned out to watch three hundred units, and the city's fountains ran green. Millions across the country recognized Saint Patrick's Day, including hundreds of thousands who marched in such places as Kansas City, Atlanta, and in Los Angeles where there were two parades, one in Hollywood, the other in Century City/Beverly Hills; both complete with film and TV stars. The Celtic influence westward from Europe did not stop at California. Across the Pacific Ocean in Japan, Tokyo's fashionable Omotesando Boulevard now has an annual Saint Patrick's Day parade, and recently included bagpipes, Celtic dancers, and four Irish wolfhounds. Tokyo also has an annual Emerald Ball, the most recent being attended by the crown prince's younger brother and his wife.

Hallmark Cards sells 150 different cards in the United States for Saint Patrick's Day, and also a T-shirt that says, "Kiss me—I'm not Irish, I just kiss good."

Typically California came up with the most extraordinary recognition of all. There a green rose was hybridized which is officially called, "Saint Patrick."

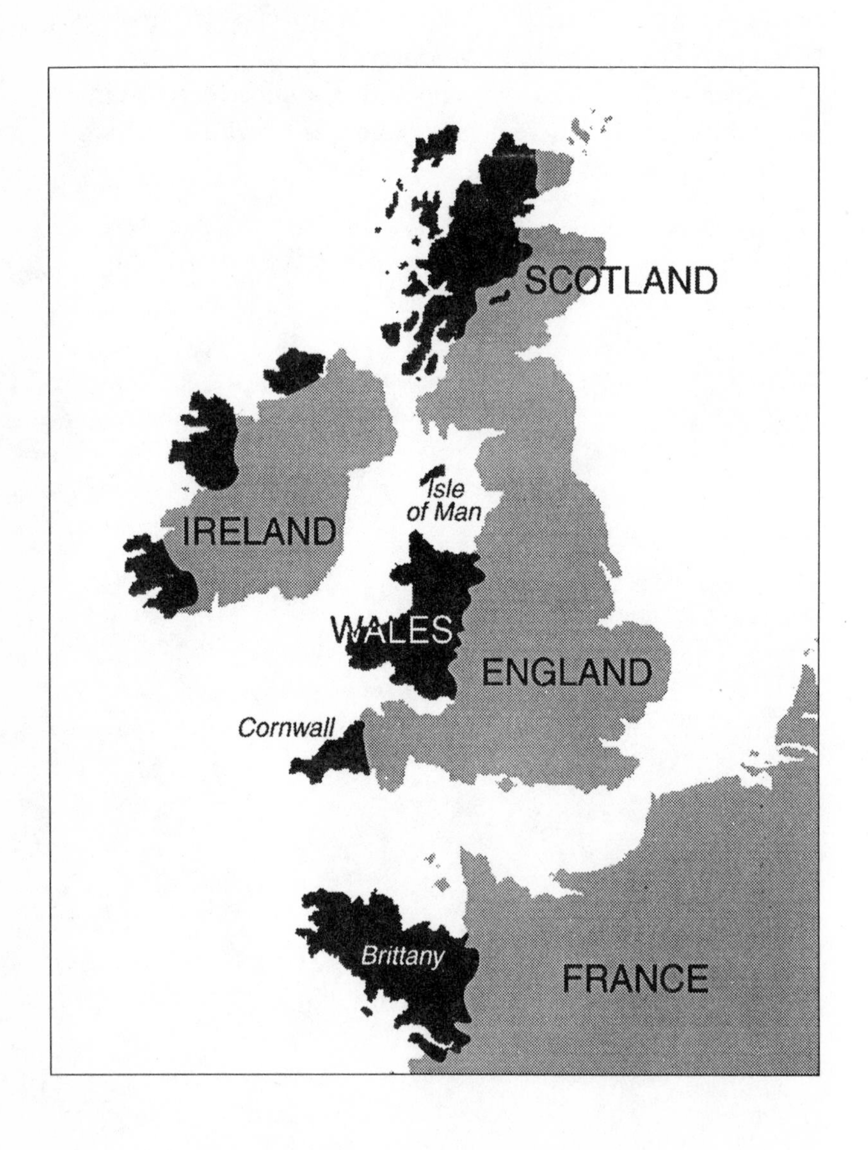

Map 2
The western fringe of Europe
where Celtic languages are still spoken.

13

The European Celts Today

The Celts who continue to maintain their identity in Europe today live along its western edge. The total Celtic population living along this "Celtic fringe" totals about fourteen million people. A Celtic language is still spoken bilingually by many in Ireland, Scotland, Wales, and France's Brittany. It is taught as an academic subject, and there are valuable libraries of Celtic literature. In other parts of the remaining Celtic world—Britain's Cornwall and the Isle of Man—there are revivals by the Cornish and the Manx to keep their Celtic heritage alive through festivals and language.

People born in this western edge of Europe who made history include such diverse figures as Robert Boyle, Henry Morton Stanley, and Dr. David Livingstone. In the seventeenth century, Irish-born chemist Robert Boyle achieved permanent recognition in the world of science for being credited with transforming alchemy into chemistry. In his original research, he initiated the practice of thoroughly describing his experiments so that anyone might repeat and confirm them. Known as the father of chemistry, millions of students on either side of the Atlantic have learned his name on being introduced to his famous "Boyle's Law" in their science classes.

The Welsh-born Celt, Sir Henry Morton Stanley, began his career as a penniless youth who emigrated to the U.S. to become a Welsh-American. While famous for finding Dr. David Livingstone in Africa for his New York paper, his greater achievement was in being the first person in history to traverse the African continent on foot from the Indian to the Atlantic Ocean. As a European he "discovered" the enormous territory that would be named the Congo (now Zaire) and gave it to Belgium.

Dr. David Livingstone was the son of poor Highlander crofting folk from the rocky island of Ulva near the once Irish settlement of Iona in Scotland. As a nineteenth-century medical doctor and missionary-turned-explorer in Africa, he added a million square miles to the known surface of the earth.

Other creative Scots include James Watt, inventor of the first effective steam engine; and winner of the Nobel prize, Alexander Fleming, the discoverer of penicillin.

The Celtic Bretons

The twentieth-century Celts in Brittany, France (many of them descendants of the Celtic Britons who fled from the Saxon invaders in Britain), formed an autonomous state within the French empire until finally annexed by France only in the ninetenth century.

In the time of Julius Caesar, "Celtic" was the language of Gaul (France) just as it was then for Britain and Ireland (and at one time or another for Switzerland, southern Germany, and many other parts of Europe.) Although in France the language of the Celts evolved into French, in its region of Brittany (*Bretagne* in French), the ancient Celtic language (*Armorican*) has survived into the twentieth century and is still proudly spoken, along with French, by 300,000 Bretons today. It is the only place in continental Europe where the Celtic language is still spoken. In an area of Portugal, however, there are still traces to be found of an archaic Celtic language, a reminder of the once enormous dimensions of the Celtic nation.

Britain Still Two-Thirds Celtic

In 1990 the Japanese formally apologized to Korea for the "hard-to-endure agony and damage" inflicted during its former colonization of that country. In 1994 the president of Germany asked forgiveness from the Polish people "for what has been done to you by Germans."

It is, however, improbable that England will ever apologize to the Celts of Wales, Scotland or Ireland for its history of aggression to those peoples. Yet the Anglo-Celtic relationship is different in some aspects from that of the Germans, Poles, Japanese and Koreans.

Although outnumbered and subjected to centuries of repression, the Celts of Britain have managed to hold on to about half of their original island into modern times (without counting traditionally Celtic Cornwall). While Wales and Scotland may include some of the most mountainous and least prosperous parts of Britain, they are considered by many to be the most beautiful and unspoiled. It is said that their inhabitants are closer to the land and are more attuned to the poetry of life. Without Wales and Scotland, Britain would be just England, and as such could not as readily call itself Great. Wales, Scotland and Cornwall, however, are not the only areas providing Britain with a Celtic population.

In 1991 the British magazine, *The Economist*, reported that "one in seven of Britain's population is either Irish by birth or linked to Ireland via parents or grandparents. There are probably more than 1 million first or second generation Irish in London alone." This report related only to the "modern" Irish Celts, and does not take into account the implications of England's Celtic heritage. It is perhaps today more appropriate than ever that the statue of the great Celtic Briton, Queen Boudicca, stands next to the Houses of

A statue of the Celtic Queen Boudicca of first-century B.C. Britain adjoins London's Houses of Parliament. Photo by author.

Queen Boudicca riding her chariot beneath London's Big Ben. Photo courtesy British Tourist Authority.

Parliament in Celtic-founded London, even if she has been erroneously called "Queen of the English" in an English history school textbook.

The Durable Scots

Some Scots survived English aggression by inhabiting the remote areas of the western Highlands and the Hebrides Islands. Many there continue to speak Gaelic and to have pride in their Celtic heritage, despite such remarkable English laws that once prohibited the Gaelic language, the Scottish kilt and the bagpipes (as an instrument of war). The infamous Highland Clearances drove Scottish people from their ancestral homes so that English gentlemen would have their land for hunting grouse and deer. In the eighteenth century, large areas in Scotland were virtually depopulated by the "enclosure" law which dispossessed Scottish tenants and left them destitute. Today there are Scots who, in a free elective process, would not have voted the English Queen Elizabeth II's Greek-born husband, Philip, to lead a royal life in London at taxpayer expense as the duke of a place called Edinburgh, the capital of Scotland.

Violent attempts by the English to annihilate cultures other than their own was a reflection of a less responsible time in human history. It *must* be progress when the English no longer consider the Gaelic language, the bagpipes or the kilt to be threatening. The present government in London provides an annual ($14.5 million) grant towards the production of Gaelic-language television programs.

To golfers everywhere, including corporate Japan, the Scots are identified with originating the game of golf (which in the Scotland of 1457 A.D. was banned in the interests of national defense). At the time of writing this book, Celtic

Ireland has the highest number of golf courses per capita (271 in total) than anywhere else in Europe.

Wales

There are modern Welsh Celts who resent the political implication intended in naming England's Prince Charles the *Prince of Wales*. The Welsh (Celtic) language is still spoken in this part of Britain despite historic attempts by the English to stifle it. The notorious Education Act of 1870 made it a requirement to hang a board bearing the words "Welsh Not" around the necks of children caught speaking Welsh at school. They were forced to wear such a sign all day and on their way home, or until they could pass it on to another child caught committing the *crime* of speaking Welsh. The humiliating plan was unsuccessful, for today Welsh is still spoken fluently with pride, bilingually with English, by about 20% of the people in that Celtic part of Britain called Wales. There has been a Welsh language revival, and for the first time in recent generations, a higher proportion of young than old people are fluent in Welsh, in part because parents have chosen to enroll their children in Welsh-medium schools which are achieving better academic results than English-medium schools. A Welsh-language TV station is popular. As in the Republic of Ireland, many public signs are bilingual—a point of national pride rather than necessity, as some of the best English in Britain is spoken in Wales (and in Scotland). The modern Welsh, perhaps to playfully confuse the English, claim to have the longest single-word place name on earth; a name so lengthy that the local railway station uses three poles to support a board displaying all of its 59 letters: *Llanfairpwllgwyngyllgogerychwyrndrobwillllantysiliogogogoch*.

The Celts Of Cornwall

Cornwall is one of the places claiming to be the land of Arthur, legendary Celtic king of Britain. Many Cornish people consider themselves to be more Celtic than English, and King Arthur may indeed have come from there to fight the Saxon invaders who would become the English. In present times, the *Lady of Flowers* and the *Grand Bard of Cornwall* are just two of the characters who take part in annual Celtic festival rites in this hauntingly lovely part of Britain called Cornwall, a place referred to by Herodotus and visited by Siculus. The revived Cornish language, *Brythonic*, is spoken by many here who may have British passports, but who proudly consider themselves Celtic. The costumes, dancing, language, and singing are a way of keeping alive these Britons' Celtic heritage. There is a Cornish Nationalist Party, and it can be considered an insult to be called an Englishman in these parts. Cornish is taught in schools along with English, and some banks will cash cheques written in Cornish. This ancient language is one of about thirty tongues given financial support by the European Bureau of Lesser Used Languages, a European Community agency in Ireland's Dublin. *Tikkidiw*, meaning butterfly, is an example of a Cornish word. It literally translates as "beautiful little thing of God."

The people of today's Cornwall live with the fact that absentee landlord and possible future king, Prince Charles, owns the valuable lands of Cornwall's most powerful private enterprise, the Duchy of Cornwall. The Prince acquired the Duchy complete with the title, Duke of Cornwall, simply by being the first-born son of Queen Elizabeth II of England's royal house of Windsor. (*Wettin*, the family name of Queen Victoria's German consort, Albert, was changed to the better-sounding *Windsor* and adopted by Britain's royal family in 1917.)

Ireland

While other European Celts are subject to the governments of Britain and France, the Celts of the Republic of Ireland (officially *Eire* in Gaelic) constitute an independent state—the only truly free Celts left in Europe. In an eight-hundred-year history of bitter rebellion and savage repression, the English have been less than successful in their attempt to subjugate Ireland. Yet up to the time of writing this book, the "Emerald Isle" was not yet entirely free of foreign rule. In Northern Ireland, the descendants of the English-planted Protestant settlers still formed a politico-religious majority which, as originally planned by the English, continued to favor being ruled by London. From 1969 to 1990, fighting between the Catholics who favor unification with the Republic of Ireland, and the Protestants, supported by armed British soldiers, has killed over three thousand people.

In the Republic of Ireland, by contrast, Protestants and Catholics have lived harmoniously together since independence was achieved from the British in 1922. The south's majority Catholics have been as friendly and religiously tolerant as any people in the world. Since independence, popular elections in the Republic of Ireland produced a Protestant president of Ireland, a Jewish mayor of Dublin, and a Catholic female president married to a Protestant. The English were permitted to continue enjoying the life of landed gentry in Ireland.

The Celts have always been known as fierce in battle but gentle in friendship. Classical writers said of the Celts that they provided hospitality and food to strangers before

A stylized Viking ship at a Dublin bus stop reflects Ireland's Viking past. Photo by Dr. Eileen Duffy.

inquiring who they were. Centuries later, in Ireland's 1742 A.D. Dublin (a city then larger than Hamburg or Berlin), the German composer Handel gave the world's first public performance of what would become his most famous and beloved work, his *Messiah.* Contrary to what he had been led to believe in London, Handel found the Irish generous and polite.

A stranger in Ireland today is still assured of "*Cead mile failte*" (a hundred thousand welcomes). Internationally, the Irish people were recently voted the most friendly to foreigners of all the people of the European Community—as polled by the European Commission and published in the French newspaper, *Liberation.* In its 1991 annual report, the United Nations Development Program ranked the world's nations in various categories of human development. These included the findings that the Republic of Ireland and Japan have the lowest murder and rape rates among all industrial nations. Dubliners were the happiest of city residents as indicated by a UNESCO survey, published in 1995, of fifteen European cities, which found that only seven percent of Dubliners would be happy about living somewhere else. Close behind in the survey were Barcelona and Copenhagen.

14

Legacy of the Celts

Progressive and highly original from their earliest beginnings, the Celts were the dominant culture north of the Alps from the sixth to the first century B.C. Their art was dazzling and unique, whether it appeared on bronze, gold, stone, bone or leather. They introduced iron into their domain and transformed it into shapes that were gracefully subtle, almost magical.

Two thousand years later, in 1991 A.D., a total of 24 nations loaned over 2,400 Celtic works to an exhibition entitled, "The Celts: The Original Europe." Hosted by Italy, the exhibition was held in the noble eighteenth century Palazzo Grassi on Venice's Grand Canal. Attracting up to 3,400 visitors a day, the year-long event was an international recognition of the importance of the Celts in history, and evidence of the appreciation that numerous countries have for the cultural and genetic legacy they inherited from the Celts.

The nations (some since changed in structure and name) loaning Celtic art and artifacts to the exhibition included Austria, Belgium, Bulgaria, Czechoslovakia, Denmark, France, Germany, Great Britain, Hungary, Ireland, Italy, Luxembourg, The Netherlands, Norway, Poland, Romania, Spain, Sweden, USA, USSR, Yugoslavia, and the Vatican. Yet works of art, however dazzling, are not for what the Celts are best known....

The Celtic Way With Words

The Celts, for more than anything else, were renowned for their sophistication of the spoken and, ultimately, the written word. This inherent ability survived nowhere more dynamically than in Ireland. It was in Ireland that many of the oral histories, folklore, mythologies, epic poems and works of art of the continental Celts survived by being passed on to the loving care of their Irish descendants, a knowledge that otherwise would have been lost forever. It was also in Ireland that a wealth of Celtic material from centuries past was at last written down, much of it to be eventually translated into other languages by well-traveled Irish monks in Britain and other parts of Europe in the centuries that followed.

The literature and scholarship of the ancient Irish Celts, despite the remoteness of their island, thus contributed impressively to the civilization of the modern world by helping to create a foundation and style for the literature of many areas in Europe which until then had little or none of their own. From the traditional learning of Celtic bards and druids there had developed in Ireland a literary heritage in the seventh, eighth and ninth centuries A.D. that stimulated intellectual activity in Europe during the Dark Ages and greatly influenced the development of medieval culture.

Imaginative Celtic myth led to King Arthur, the (druid) wizard Merlin, Camelot, Tristan and Isolde, the Holy Grail, the concept of chivalry and the countless stories it spawned. A great body of European literature thus owes its existence to the Celts, and to the Celts of Ireland in particular. Surviving original manuscripts of ancient Irish literature, the oldest in Europe after Greek and Latin, can be found in the libraries and museums of various countries today. Scotland and Wales produced such men of the pen as Robert Burns, Sir Walter

Scott, Robert Louis Stevenson, and Dylan Thomas, but only in Ireland was there a strong continuity linking the rich traditions of the ancient Celtic past with the modern writer.

In Ireland, the connection between the earliest Celtic literature and that of Irish writers in more recent times can be seen in a mutual love of satire, language, and the complex saga, which James Joyce, for instance, kept alive in some of his famous written works, particularly in *Finnegan's Wake*. In Dublin, two hundred years earlier, Irish-born Jonathan Swift's biting satire directed at the inhuman English policies in Ireland would have qualified him as a Celtic bard in ancient times.

More recent Irish writers include Liam O'Flaherty, Sean O'Faolain, Frank O'Connor, Maeve Brennan, Patrick Kavanagh, Mary Lavin, Lady Gregory, George Moore, Seumas O'Kelly, James Stephen, James Plunkett, Sean O'Casey, Samuel Beckett, Edna O'Brien, George Bernard Shaw, and Oscar Wilde (whose full name was Oscar Fingall O'Flahertie Wills Wilde). Seamus Heaney even more recently contributed to the internationally renowned reputation of the Irish for words, wit and writing. This Irishman was awarded the 1995 Nobel prize in literature (and a million dollars). Leading up to that event, he taught at the University of California at Berkeley, was professor of poetry at England's Oxford University for five years, and from 1985 has been back in the United States as professor of rhetoric at Harvard University.

Another Irish poet, William Butler Yeats, born in Dublin 1865, was awarded the 1923 Nobel prize in literature—just before Irish-born-and-bred George Bernard Shaw received his in 1925. Irishman Samuel Beckett won his Nobel prize in literature in 1969. Earlier, across the Atlantic, Irish American writer, Eugene O'Neill, received his Nobel award in 1936.

American writers of Irish descent do not always have names as obviously Celtic as O'Neill, or those possessed, for example, by Flannery O'Connor, Mary McCarthy, J.P. Dunleavy and Tom Clancy.

William James, the Irish-born progenitor of a renowned Irish American family, migrated across the Atlantic from a tenant farm in Ireland in 1786 to become one of the wealthiest men in America. He ultimately left behind him the literary legacy of his grandson, Henry James, whose numerous novels include *The American*, *Daisy Miller*, *The Portrait Of A Lady*, *The Bostonians*, *The Turn Of The Screw*, *The Wings Of The Dove*, *The Ambassadors*, and *The Golden Bowl*. James, who also wrote three autobiographical works and several books on travel, is, however, especially known for his literary criticism which earned him an international and permanent reputation as a master technician in the literary world.

In her novel, *Gone With The Wind*, Margaret Mitchell recognized her Celtic origins by creating a second Tara in America for her green-eyed Irish heroine, Scarlett O'Hara. The original Tara is a place in Ireland from where Irish kings once ruled. Margaret Mitchell's Irish ancestor came from Tipperary in Ireland. Her book, said to be the world's most famous novel, has sold 25 million copies, and still sells 40,000 hard-cover copies a year a half century after its initial publication. In 1991 a sequel was written and published by people Mitchell would never know—after the rights had been bought from her heirs, two nephews, for five million dollars.

Perhaps no Irish writer anywhere has received more attention than James Joyce. His internationally renowned *Ulysses* is considered to be the twentieth century's most celebrated literary masterpiece. In 1984, Hans Walter Gabler, professor of English at the University of Munich, published *Ulysses: The Corrected Text*. The cost of his seven-year study of Joyce's *Ulysses* was paid for with a $300,000 grant from the German government. The James Joyce Research Center at Boston University has 250 separate editions of *Ulysses*. About two hundred articles on Joyce are written each year—published in six different journals devoted exclusively to publishing *Joyceana*. Yet another journal is needed for the reviews of the twenty to thirty new books that come out each year about Joyce. The annual James Joyce Symposium held by the University of California at Irvine in 1993 attracted hundreds of scholars and was focused on "Joyce and Culture." Papers and panels included works by Joyce authorities from Ireland, England, Canada, Scotland, France, Germany, Switzerland, the Netherlands, Austria, Indonesia and the U.S. Registrants included Joyce scholars from Latvia, Brazil, Russia and China. Though skilled at conventional writing, Joyce is famous for abandoning plot and presenting to his readers random incidents that are slices of life—as in his earliest fiction, *Dubliners*. His masterpiece, *Ulysses*, (which was once banned in the United States), is about the events of a single day in the Dublin of Joyce's youth. Joyce attended a school run by the Catholic Jesuits near Dublin and would later say that to understand him you would have to understand the Jesuits. Perhaps coincidentally, the Scottish creator of the sleuthing Sherlock Holmes, Sir Arthur Conan Doyle (whose grandfather was born in Dublin) was also schooled by the Jesuits.

Yeats, along with fellow Irish writers Lady Augusta Gregory, John Synge and others were active in the early days of Dublin's Abbey Theatre. They wrote plays for modern audiences based on the ancient Celtic manuscripts that had been researched with loving care by Standish O'Grady. This scholar wrote what could be called an Irish Book of Genesis—essentially a popular history of Ireland from the first to the fourth centuries A.D. when neighboring Celtic

Britain was occupied by the Romans (and before the Saxons and other Germanic tribes invaded that island to become the rudimentary English). This ancient history featured the legendary and greatest of all Irish heroes, *Cuchulainn*, along with the *Fir Bolgs*, the *Fomoiri*, and the *Milesians*.

A different kind of fame is attached to Irish-born writer Bram Stoker who wrote the original gothic horror tale of the vampire Count Dracula, a novel since repeatedly adapted for stage and screen. As a child, Stoker's mother told him stories of the 1832 cholera epidemic in the west of Ireland in which some cholera victims, presumed dead, were said to have stirred back to life in their open coffins. These childhood stories, along with *Carmilla*, a vampire story written by another Irish writer, Sheridan Le Fanu, are said to have been the inspiration for Stoker's *Dracula* (which he initially named *The Undead*). Stoker was probably unaware of the coincidence that the earliest Celtic-made coins, showing mythological symbols, were struck in the region now known as Transylvania when Celts lived in that part of Europe a couple of thousand years earlier—well before the concept of a state called Romania.

A Three-Thousand-Year History That Includes Rock And Roll

Classical historians referred to the Celts' way with words, and the same early Celts' interest in music has been indicated by seventh-century B.C. Celtic-made pottery ornamented with dancing figures and musical instruments found in Hungary. Perhaps the music of Ireland's internationally famous, traditional music ensemble, The Chieftains, best represents Celtic music as it was played over the centuries with its powerful themes of grief, loneliness, exaltation, warmth and love. Successfully combining the best of folk and classical musical traditions, The Chieftains have played to sold-out concerts worldwide. Their leader, Paddy Maloney, wrote musical scores for major American theatrical feature films.

The Celts have always loved language and music, and both contributed to the modern phenomenon known as *Celtic Rock*. In the highly competitive world of rock and pop music, the Republic of Ireland, with a total population of only 3.8 million, continues to produce internationally acclaimed performers and groups known as much for their philosophical lyrics as for their music. Sinead O'Connor was described by *Rolling Stone* magazine as the "first pop superstar of the 90's" even before she won the best video award and two other top honors at the MTV Music Awards against glittering competition at the Universal Amphitheatre in Los Angeles. Representing America's top video awards, the show was televised in 100 countries around the world. The Irish rock group known as U2, often called the world's most successful rock band, made the cover of *Time* magazine and was voted by *Rolling Stone* magazine as having the world's best artist, best band, best album, best single, and best video of the year. U2 signed a $60-million-plus record contract, making them the world's highest paid group. Another preeminent band from Ireland, Altan, has become internationally famous for its traditional Irish music, with albums consistently rising to the tops of world music charts. Its founder/leader, Mairead Ni Mhaonaigh, is a young woman who sings primarily in Gaelic, the Celtic language called Irish by the Irish.

But then good music could always be heard among the Celts in Wales, Scotland, and Ireland, from the fiddler at the local pub to the social gatherings in the remotest villages. Even the poorest Celts on their way across the Atlantic in the immigrant "coffin ships" were entertained and cheered by irrepressible fiddlers among them. They could not have known that generations later, in 1996, an American astronaut and fellow Celt named Brian Duffy would command the U.S. spacecraft *Endeavour* high above the Atlantic as he helped lead the way into the twenty-first century at more than 28,000 kilometers per hour.

The Durable Celts

For millennia the Celts have known their share of war and famine, yet they are still around. Their passion for personal freedom is at the very core of their nature. This respect for individuality may not have served them well in fighting Rome's single-minded legions, but it represented an early consciousness of human rights that has only recently become fashionable in democratic nations of the modern world.

BIBLIOGRAPHY

Bakeless, J. and K. *Signers of the Declaration*. Houghton Mifflin, 1969.

Bayerisches Landesamt Für Denkmalpflege. *Schatze Aus Bayerns Erde* (Treasures from Bavarian Soil). 1983.

Beer, Lorentz, ed. *Heiligenlegende* (Legends of the Saints). Regensburg, Germany. 1913, 1914, 1939.

Biel, Jorg. *Der Keltenfürst von Hochdorf* (The Celtic Duke of Hochdorf). Germany. 1985.

Bieler, Ludwig. *Ireland: Harbinger of the Middle Ages*. Oxford University Press, 1963.

Birmingham, Stephen. *Real Lace: America's Irish Rich*. Harper and Row, 1973.

Bonwick, James. *Irish Druids and Old Irish Religions*. 1894. Dorset Press edition, 1986.

Bowen, E.G. *Saints, Seaways and Settlements in the Celtic Islands*. University of Wales Press, 1969.

Brogan, Olwen. *Roman Gaul*. Harvard University Press, 1953.

Brengle, L. Richard, ed. *Arthur, King of Britain*. New York: Appleton-Century-Crofts, 1964.

Caesar, Julius. *The Gallic War*. Translated by H.J. Edwards. Harvard University Press, 1966.

Cottrell, Leonard. *The Great Invasion*. London: Evans Brothers Ltd., 1958.

Cunliffe, Barry. *The Celtic World*. McGraw-Hill, 1979.

Chadwick, Nora. *The Celts*. Penguin, 1991.

Chadwick, Nora. *Celtic Britain*. Frederick A. Praeger, 1963.

Duft, Johannes. *The Abbey Library of St. Gall*. Stiftsbibliothek Sankt Gallen. Switzerland, 1982.

Ellis, Peter Berresford. *Caesar's Invasion of Britain*. New York University Press, 1980.

Ellis, Peter Berresford. *The Celtic Empire, The First Millennium of Celtic History; 1000 B.C. - 51 A.D.* Carolina Academic Press, 1990.

Ellis, Peter Berresford. *Hell or Connaught!* London: Hamish Hamilton, 1975.

Filip, Jan. *Celtic Civilization and Its Heritage*. Prague: 1977.

Fuller, J.F.C. *Julius Caesar: Man, Soldier and Tyrant*. Eyre and Spottiswoode, 1965.

Green, Miranda, J. *Dictionary of Celtic Myth and Legend*. Thames and Hudson, 1992.

Snodgrass, Mary Ellen. *Roman Classics*. Cliffs Notes, 1988.

Jackson, Kenneth. *A Celtic Miscellany: Translations from the Celtic Literatures*. Dorset Press, 1986.

Kee, Robert. *Ireland, A History*. London: Weidenfeld and Nicolson, 1980.

Kruta, Venceslas; Frey, Otto Herman; Szabo, Miklos; Raftery, Barry, eds. *The Celts*. 799 pages. Milan, Italy: Bompiani, 1991.

Livy. *The Early History of Rome*. Translated by Aubrey de Selincourt, 1973.

McNally, Robert. *Old Ireland*. Fordham University Press, 1965.

Mohen, Jean-Pierre. *The World of Megaliths*. Facts On File, 1990.

Newark, Tim. *Celtic Warriors*. Blandford Press, 1986.

Piggott, Stuart. *Ancient Europe*. Aldine Press, 1965.

Piggott, Stuart. *The Druids*. Thames and Hudson, 1986.

Polybius. *Polybius, Histories*. Translated by W.R. Paton, 1922.

Powell, T.G.E. *The Celts*. Thames and Hudson, 1986.

Raftery, Joseph, ed. *The Celts*. Mercier Press, 1967.

Raftery, Barry. *Pagan Celtic Ireland*. Thames and Hudson, 1994.

Ross, Anne. *Pagan Celtic Britain*. Routledge and Kegan Paul, 1967.

Ross, Anne. *Everyday Life of the Pagan Celts*. Putnam, 1970.

Ross, A., and Robins, D. *The Life and Death of a Druid Prince*. Summit/Simon and Schuster, 1989.

Rutherford, Ward. *The Druids and Their Heritage*. London: Gordon and Cremonesi, 1978.

Severin, T. *The Brendan Voyage*. London: 1978.

Szabo, M. *The Celtic Heritage in Hungary*. Budapest: 1971.

Thomas, Stanley. *Pre-Roman Britain*. Connecticut: New York Graphic Society Publishers, Ltd., 1965.

Tierney, J.J. *The Celtic Ethnography of Posidonius*. Proceedings of the Royal Irish Academy, 1960.

Wilson, D., ed. *The Northern World*. New York: Harry N. Abrams, 1990.

INDEX